interchange

FIFTH EDITION

3

Student's Book

Jack C. Richards
with Jonathan Hull and Susan Proctor

WITH DIGITAL PACK

CAMBRIDGE
UNIVERSITY PRESS

CAMBRIDGE
UNIVERSITY PRESS

University Printing House, Cambridge CB2 8BS, United Kingdom

One Liberty Plaza, 20th Floor, New York, NY 10006, USA

477 Williamstown Road, Port Melbourne, VIC 3207, Australia

314–321, 3rd Floor, Plot 3, Splendor Forum, Jasola District Centre, New Delhi – 110025, India

103 Penang Road, #05-06/07, Visioncrest Commercial, Singapore 238467

Torre de los Parques, Colonia Tlacoquemécatl del Valle, Mexico City CP 03200, Mexico

Cambridge University Press is part of the University of Cambridge.

It furthers the University's mission by disseminating knowledge in the pursuit of education, learning and research at the highest international levels of excellence.

www.cambridge.org
Information on this title: www.cambridge.org/9781009040754

First published 2013
Fifth edition 2017
Fifth edition update published 2021

20 19 18 17 16 15 14 13 12 11

Printed in Poland by Opolgraf

A catalogue record for this publication is available from the British Library

ISBN 978-1-009-04052-5 Student's Book 3 with eBook
ISBN 978-1-009-04053-2 Student's Book 3A with eBook
ISBN 978-1-009-04054-9 Student's Book 3B with eBook
ISBN 978-1-009-04075-4 Student's Book 3 with Digital Pack
ISBN 978-1-009-04077-8 Student's Book 3A with Digital Pack
ISBN 978-1-009-04078-5 Student's Book 3B with Digital Pack
ISBN 978-1-316-62276-6 Workbook 3
ISBN 978-1-316-62277-3 Workbook 3A
ISBN 978-1-316-62279-7 Workbook 3B
ISBN 978-1-108-40711-3 Teacher's Edition 3
ISBN 978-1-316-62230-8 Class Audio 3
ISBN 978-1-009-04079-2 Full Contact 3 with Digital Pack
ISBN 978-1-009-04080-8 Full Contact 3A with Digital Pack
ISBN 978-1-009-04081-5 Full Contact 3B with Digital Pack
ISBN 978-1-108-40307-8 Presentation Plus 3

Additional resources for this publication at cambridgeone.org

Informed by teachers

Teachers from all over the world helped develop *Interchange Fifth Edition.* They looked at everything – from the color of the designs to the topics in the conversations – in order to make sure that this course will work in the classroom. We heard from 1,500 teachers in:

- Surveys
- Focus Groups
- In-Depth Reviews

We appreciate the help and input from everyone. In particular, we'd like to give the following people our special thanks:

Jader Franceschi, **Actúa Idiomas,** Bento Gonçalves, Rio Grande do Sul, Brazil
Juliana Dos Santos Voltan Costa, **Actus Idiomas,** São Paulo, Brazil
Ella Osorio, **Angelo State University,** San Angelo, TX, US
Mary Hunter, **Angelo State University,** San Angelo, TX, US
Mario César González, **Angloamericano de Monterrey, SC,** Monterrey, Mexico
Samantha Shipman, **Auburn High School,** Auburn, AL, US
Linda, **Bernick Language School,** Radford, VA, US
Dave Lowrance, **Bethesda University of California,** Yorba Linda, CA, US
Tajbakhsh Hosseini**, Bezmialem Vakif University,** Istanbul, Turkey
Dilek Gercek, **Bil English,** Izmir, Turkey
Erkan Kolat, **Biruni University, ELT,** Istanbul, Turkey
Nika Gutkowska, **Bluedata International,** New York, NY, US
Daniel Alcocer Gómez, **Cecatl 92,** Guadalupe, Nuevo León, Mexico
Samantha Webb, **Central Middle School,** Milton-Freewater, OR, US
Verónica Salgado, **Centro Anglo Americano,** Cuernavaca, Mexico
Ana Rivadeneira Martínez and Georgia P. de Machuca, **Centro de Educación Continua – Universidad Politécnica del Ecuador,** Quito, Ecuador
Anderson Francisco Guimerães Maia, **Centro Cultural Brasil Estados Unidos,** Belém, Brazil
Rosana Mariano, **Centro Paula Souza,** São Paulo, Brazil
Carlos de la Paz Arroyo, Teresa Noemí Parra Alarcón, Gilberto
Bastida Gaytan, Manuel Esquivel Román, and Rosa Cepeda Tapia, **Centro Universitario Angloamericano,** Cuernavaca, Morelos, Mexico
Antonio Almeida, **CETEC,** Morelos, Mexico
Cinthia Ferreira, **Cinthia Ferreira Languages Services,** Toronto, ON, Canada
Phil Thomas and Sérgio Sanchez, **CLS Canadian Language School,** São Paulo, Brazil
Celia Concannon, **Cochise College,** Nogales, AZ, US
Maria do Carmo Rocha and CAOP English team, **Colégio Arquidiocesano Ouro Preto – Unidade Cônego Paulo Dilascio,** Ouro Preto, Brazil
Kim Rodriguez, **College of Charleston North,** Charleston, SC, US
Jesús Leza Alvarado, **Coparmex English Institute,** Monterrey, Mexico
John Partain, **Cortazar,** Guanajuato, Mexico
Alexander Palencia Navas, **Cursos de Lenguas, Universidad del Atlántico,** Barranquilla, Colombia
Kenneth Johan Gerardo Steenhuisen Cera, Melfi Osvaldo Guzman Triana, and Carlos Alberto Algarín Jiminez, **Cursos de Lenguas Extranjeras Universidad del Atlantico,** Barranquilla, Colombia
Jane P Kerford, **East Los Angeles College,** Pasadena, CA, US
Daniela, **East Village,** Campinas, São Paulo, Brazil
Rosalva Camacho Orduño, **Easy English for Groups S.A. de C.V.,** Monterrey, Nuevo León, Mexico
Adonis Gimenez Fusetti, **Easy Way Idiomas,** Ibiúna, Brazil
Eileen Thompson, **Edison Community College,** Piqua, OH, US
Ahminne Handeri O.L Froede, **Englishouse escola de idiomas,** Teófilo Otoni, Brazil
Ana Luz Delgado-Izazola, **Escuela Nacional Preparatoria 5, UNAM,** Mexico City, Mexico
Nancy Alarcón Mendoza, **Facultad de Estudios Superiores Zaragoza, UNAM,** Mexico City, Mexico
Marcilio N. Barros, **Fast English USA,** Campinas, São Paulo, Brazil
Greta Douthat, **FCI Ashland,** Ashland, KY, US
Carlos Lizárraga González, **Grupo Educativo Anglo Americano, S.C.,** Mexico City, Mexico
Hugo Fernando Alcántar Valle, **Instituto Politécnico Nacional, Escuela Superior de Comercio y Administración-Unidad Santotomás, Celex Esca Santo Tomás,** Mexico City, Mexico
Sueli Nascimento, **Instituto Superior de Educação do Rio de Janeiro,** Rio de Janeiro, Brazil
Elsa F Monteverde, **International Academic Services,** Miami, FL, US
Laura Anand, **Irvine Adult School,** Irvine, CA, US
Prof. Marli T. Fernandes (principal) and Prof. Dr. Jefferson J. Fernandes (pedagogue), **Jefferson Idiomass,** São Paulo, Brazil
Herman Bartelen, **Kanda Gaigo Gakuin,** Tokyo, Japan
Cassia Silva, **Key Languages,** Key Biscayne, FL, US
Sister Mary Hope, **Kyoto Notre Dame Joshi Gakuin,** Kyoto, Japan
Nate Freedman, **LAL Language Centres,** Boston, MA, US
Richard Janzen, **Langley Secondary School,** Abbotsford, BC, Canada

Christina Abel Gabardo, **Language House,** Campo Largo, Brazil

Ivonne Castro, **Learn English International,** Cali, Colombia

Julio Cesar Maciel Rodrigues, **Liberty Centro de Línguas,** São Paulo, Brazil

Ann Gibson, **Maynard High School,** Maynard, MA, US

Martin Darling, **Meiji Gakuin Daigaku,** Tokyo, Japan

Dax Thomas, **Meiji Gakuin Daigaku,** Yokohama, Kanagawa, Japan

Derya Budak, **Mevlana University,** Konya, Turkey

B Sullivan, **Miami Valley Career Technical Center International Program,** Dayton, OH, US

Julio Velazquez, **Milo Language Center,** Weston, FL, US

Daiane Siqueira da Silva, Luiz Carlos Buontempo, Marlete Avelina de Oliveira Cunha, Marcos Paulo Segatti, Morgana Eveline de Oliveira, Nadia Lia Gino Alo, and Paul Hyde Budgen, **New Interchange-Escola de Idiomas,** São Paulo, Brazil

Patrícia França Furtado da Costa, Juiz de Fora, Brazil

Patricia Servín

Chris Pollard, **North West Regional College SK,** North Battleford, SK, Canada

Olga Amy, **Notre Dame High School,** Red Deer, Canada

Amy Garrett, **Ouachita Baptist University,** Arkadelphia, AR, US

Mervin Curry, **Palm Beach State College,** Boca Raton, FL, US

Julie Barros, **Quality English Studio,** Guarulhos, São Paulo, Brazil

Teodoro González Saldaña and Jesús Monserrrta Mata Franco, **Race Idiomas,** Mexico City, Mexico

Autumn Westphal and Noga La`or, **Rennert International,** New York, NY, US

Antonio Gallo and Javy Palau, **Rigby Idiomas,** Monterrey, Mexico Tatiane Gabriela Sperb do Nascimento, **Right Way,** Igrejinha, Brazil

Mustafa Akgül, **Selahaddin Eyyubi Universitesi,** Diyarbakır, Turkey

James Drury M. Fonseca, **Senac Idiomas Fortaleza,** Fortaleza, Ceara, Brazil

Manoel Fialho S Neto, **Senac – PE,** Recife, Brazil

Jane Imber, **Small World,** Lawrence, KS, US

Tony Torres, **South Texas College,** McAllen, TX, US

Janet Rose, **Tennessee Foreign Language Institute,** College Grove, TN, US

Todd Enslen, **Tohoku University,** Sendai, Miyagi, Japan

Daniel Murray, **Torrance Adult School,** Torrance, CA, US

Juan Manuel Pulido Mendoza, **Universidad del Atlántico,** Barranquilla, Colombia

Juan Carlos Vargas Millán, **Universidad Libre Seccional Cali,** Cali (Valle del Cauca), Colombia

Carmen Cecilia Llanos Ospina, **Universidad Libre Seccional Cali,** Cali, Colombia

Jorge Noriega Zenteno, **Universidad Politécnica del Valle de México,** Estado de México, Mexico

Aimee Natasha Holguin S., **Universidad Politécnica del Valle de México UPVM,** Tultitlàn Estado de México, Mexico

Christian Selene Bernal Barraza, **UPVM Universidad Politécnica del Valle de México,** Ecatepec, Mexico

Lizeth Ramos Acosta, **Universidad Santiago de Cali,** Cali, Colombia

Silvana Dushku, **University of Illinois Champaign,** IL, US

Deirdre McMurtry, **University of Nebraska – Omaha,** Omaha, NE, US

Jason E Mower, **University of Utah,** Salt Lake City, UT, US

Paul Chugg, **Vanguard Taylor Language Institute,** Edmonton, Alberta, Canada

Henry Mulak, **Varsity Tutors,** Los Angeles, CA, US

Shirlei Strucker Calgaro and Hugo Guilherme Karrer, **VIP Centro de Idiomas,** Panambi, Rio Grande do Sul, Brazil

Eleanor Kelly, **Waseda Daigaku Extension Centre,** Tokyo, Japan

Sherry Ashworth, **Wichita State University,** Wichita, KS, US

Laine Bourdene, **William Carey University,** Hattiesburg, MS, US

Serap Aydın, Istanbul, Turkey

Liliana Covino, Guarulhos, Brazil

Yannuarys Jiménez, Barranquilla, Colombia

Juliana Morais Pazzini, Toronto, ON, Canada

Marlon Sanches, Montreal, Canada

Additional content contributed by Kenna Bourke, Inara Couto, Nic Harris, Greg Manin, Ashleigh Martinez, Laura McKenzie, Paul McIntyre, Clara Prado, Lynne Robertson, Mari Vargo, Theo Walker, and Maria Lucia Zaorob.

Classroom Language Student questions

Plan of Book 3

1 That's my kind of friend!

- Discuss personalities and qualities
- Discuss likes and dislikes

1 SNAPSHOT

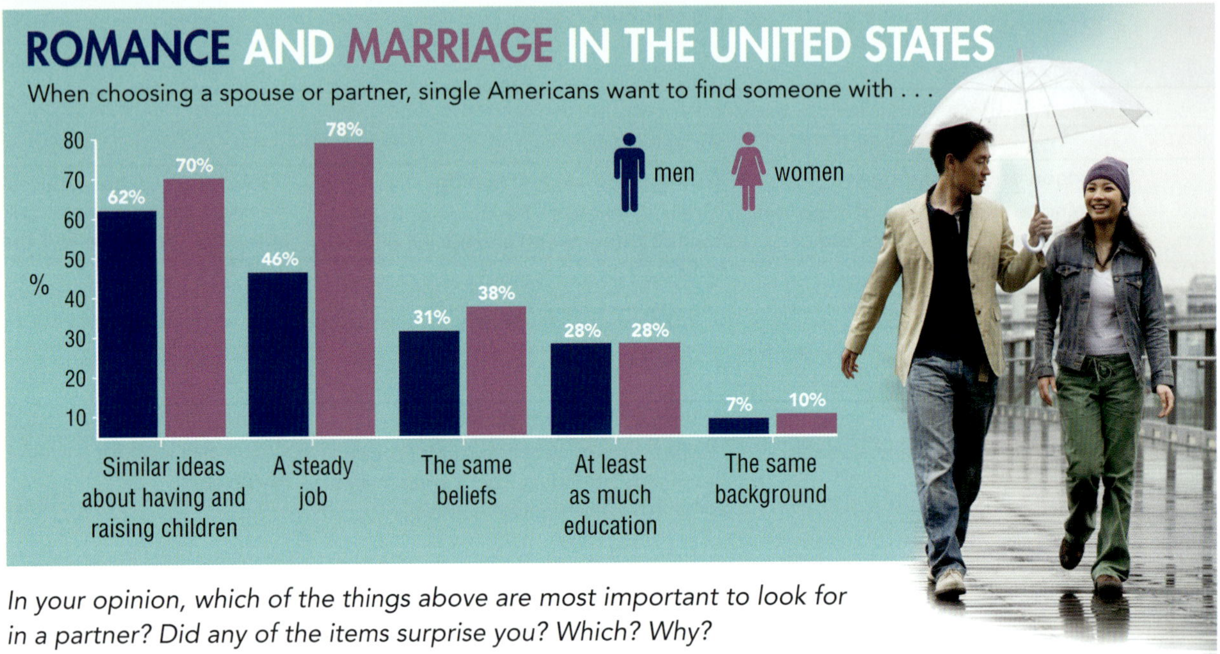

In your opinion, which of the things above are most important to look for in a partner? Did any of the items surprise you? Which? Why? Are there other important qualities missing from the list?

2 CONVERSATION What *are* you looking for?

A Listen and practice.

Joe: What are you doing?

Roy: I'm setting up my profile for this online dating site. I have to describe the kind of person I'm looking for.

Joe: I see. And what are you looking for?

Roy: Oh, I like people who aren't too serious and who have a good sense of humor. You know, someone I can have fun with.

Joe: OK. Uh, what else?

Roy: Well, I'd like someone I have something in common with – who I can talk to easily.

Joe: I think I know just the girl for you: my cousin Lisa. She's a lot of fun and she loves sports, just like you.

Roy: Well, why not? I'll give it a try.

Joe: OK, I'll invite her over for dinner, and you can tell me what you think.

B Listen to Joe and Roy discuss Lisa after they had dinner together. What did Roy think of her?

3 GRAMMAR FOCUS

Relative pronouns

As the subject of a clause	As the object of a clause
I like people **who/that** aren't too serious.	I want someone **(who/that)** I can have fun with.
I like people **who/that** have a good sense of humor.	I'd like someone **(who/that)** I can talk to easily.

GRAMMAR PLUS *see page 132*

A Match the information in columns A and B. Then compare with a partner.

A	B
1. I don't like to work with people who/that __c__	**a.** help me understand things easily.
2. I have some good, old friends who/that _____	**b.** is messy.
3. I discuss my problems with people who/that _____	**c.** are too competitive.
4. I don't want to have a roommate who/that _____	**d.** I can respect as a leader.
5. I'd like to have a boss who/that _____	**e.** I met in middle school.
6. I enjoy teachers who/that _____	**f.** I have a lot in common with.
7. I'm looking for a partner who/that _____	**g.** can give me good advice.

B Put a line through *who/that* in part A if it's optional. Then compare with a partner.

C **PAIR WORK** Complete the sentences in column A with your own information. Do you and your partner have similar opinions?

A: I don't like to work with people who are too competitive.
B: Neither do I. I like to work with people who are friendly and helpful.

4 WORD POWER Personality traits

A Match the words with the definitions. Then decide whether the words are positive (**P**) or negative (**N**). Write **P** or **N** after each word.

__h__	**1.** easygoing __P__	**a.** a person who doesn't change easily and is stubborn
_____	**2.** egotistical _____	**b.** someone who doesn't like giving or spending money
_____	**3.** inflexible _____	**c.** someone who has a very high opinion of him- or herself
_____	**4.** modest _____	**d.** someone who is helpful and encouraging
_____	**5.** outgoing _____	**e.** a person who doesn't do what he or she promised
_____	**6.** stingy _____	**f.** a person who enjoys being with other people
_____	**7.** supportive _____	**g.** a person who has unpredictable or irregular moods
_____	**8.** temperamental _____	**h.** a person who doesn't worry much or get angry easily
_____	**9.** unreliable _____	**i.** someone who doesn't brag about his or her accomplishments

B **PAIR WORK** Cover the definitions. Take turns talking about the adjectives in your own words.

"An easygoing person is someone who . . ."

C **PAIR WORK** Think of at least two adjectives to describe your favorite relative. Then tell a partner.

5 LISTENING What's new?

A Listen to conversations that describe three people. Are the descriptions positive (**P**) or negative (**N**)? Check (✓) the box.

1. Emma	☐ P	☐ N		
2. Mrs. Leblanc	☐ P	☐ N		
3. Pablo	☐ P	☐ N		

B Listen again. Write two adjectives that describe each person in the chart.

6 DISCUSSION The right qualities

A What is the ideal friend, parent, or partner like? Add your own type of person under **People**. Then write one quality each ideal person should have, and one each should *not* have.

People	This person is . . .	This person is not . . .
The ideal friend		
The ideal parent		
The ideal partner		
The ideal ________		

B **GROUP WORK** Take turns describing your ideal people. Try to agree on the two most important qualities for each person.

A: I think the ideal friend is someone who is supportive and who is a good listener.
B: I agree. The ideal friend is someone who isn't critical . . .
C: Oh, I'm not sure I agree. . . .

7 WRITING A good friend

A Think about a good friend. Answer the questions. Then write a paragraph.

What is this person like?
How long have you known each other?
How did you meet?
How are you similar?
How are you different?
What makes your relationship special?

My friend Nolan is easygoing and doesn't take life too seriously. He's someone who loves to have fun, and he makes sure everyone else has a good time, too. We met about six years ago . . .

B **PAIR WORK** Exchange paragraphs. How are your friends similar? How are they different?

8 PERSPECTIVES Are you difficult to please?

A Listen to some common complaints. Check (✓) the ones you agree with.

Do you get ANNOYED easily? Take the quiz and find out.

- ☐ I can't stand it when a child screams in a restaurant.
- ☐ I can't stand it when I'm upset and people tell me to calm down.
- ☐ It bothers me when my doctor arrives late for an appointment.
- ☐ I don't like it when someone takes the last cookie without asking.
- ☐ It upsets me when a close friend forgets my birthday.
- ☐ I don't like it when people call me early in the morning on the weekend just to chat.
- ☐ It bothers me when a friend answers the phone at the dinner table.
- ☐ I hate it when people text the message "Call me."

Score: If you checked . . .

1–2 complaints: Wow! You don't get annoyed very easily.
3–4 complaints: You're fairly easygoing.
5–6 complaints: You get irritated pretty easily.
7–8 complaints: Relax! You get upset too easily.

B Calculate your score. Do you get annoyed easily? Tell the class what bothers you the most.

9 PRONUNCIATION Linked sounds

A Listen and practice. Final consonant sounds are often linked to the vowel sounds that follow them.

It‿upsets me when‿a friend‿is late for‿an‿appointment.
I love‿it when‿a friend‿is supportive‿and kind.

B Mark the linked sounds in the sentences below. Listen and check. Then practice saying the sentences.

1. I hate it when a cell phone goes off at the movies.
2. I can't stand it when a person is inflexible.
3. Does it bother you when a friend is unreliable?

C **PAIR WORK** Take turns saying the sentences in Exercise 8. Pay attention to linked sounds.

10 GRAMMAR FOCUS

It clauses + adverbial clauses with *when*

I like **it**	**when** my roommate cleans the apartment.
I don't mind **it**	**when** a friend answers the phone at the dinner table.
I can't stand **it**	**when** I'm upset and people tell me to calm down.
It makes me happy	**when** people do nice things for no reason.
It bothers me	**when** my doctor arrives late for an appointment.
It upsets me	**when** a close friend forgets my birthday.

GRAMMAR PLUS *see page 132*

A How do you feel about these situations? Complete the sentences with *it* clauses from the list. Then compare your sentences with a partner.

I love it	**I don't mind it**	**It annoys me**	**It really upsets me**
I like it	**It doesn't bother me**	**I don't like it**	**I can't stand it**
It makes me happy	**I hate it**		

1. ______________________ when a friend gives me a present for no special reason.
2. ______________________ when someone criticizes a friend of mine.
3. ______________________ when friends start arguing in front of me.
4. ______________________ when people call me late at night.
5. ______________________ when salesclerks are temperamental.
6. ______________________ when people are direct and say what's on their mind.
7. ______________________ when someone corrects my grammar in front of others.
8. ______________________ when a friend is sensitive and supportive.
9. ______________________ when people throw trash on the ground.
10. ______________________ when a friend treats me to dinner.

B **GROUP WORK** Do you ever get annoyed by a certain type of person or situation? Write down five things that annoy you the most. Then compare in groups.

A: I can't stand it when someone takes food off my plate.
B: I feel the same way. Especially when the person didn't order his or her own food!
C: Yeah, but it bothers me more when . . .

11 INTERCHANGE 1 Personality quiz

Interview a classmate to find out about his or her personality.
Go to Interchange 1 on page 114.

12 READING

A Are you a frequent social media user? What kinds of things get your attention on social media?

HOME NEWS ABOUT CULTURE

SOCIAL NETWORKS THAT AREN'T FOR EVERYONE

Since social networking websites first appeared, many have come and some have gone. However, their purpose has generally been the same: keeping up with old friends, making new friends, and sharing pictures, videos, and bits of interesting news. In addition, some sites make it possible to pursue new relationships, either online or in the real world.

For some people who have very specific interests, generic sites like Facebook or Twitter are not sufficient. They want to be part of a supportive online community that shares their particular passions.

A good example is Stache Passions, a social site for people who wear, admire, or have an interest in moustaches. It features photos of men with all sizes and styles of moustaches, forums for discussing the history, growing, and styling of the 'stache, and even a meet-up page to help you meet other moustache-lovers.

Pursonals is a specialized site for those who love cats. Here you can meet and chat with cat-loving friends, set up feline play-dates with local people and their pets, and even find a home for a cat in need. And if your friends don't like it when you share endless cute cat videos on your regular social site, Pursonals is where people are sure to appreciate them!

On a more serious note, Horyou is a website for people that want to do good in the world. On the site, you can connect with other social activists and entrepreneurs, plan meetings, share fund-raising strategies, and keep up with thousands of people who are working hard to make the world a better place. There are no funny videos here, but Horyou offers its own web-based video channel that features programs and documentaries about efforts to improve people's lives around the globe.

B Read the article. Which website is good for the people below? Write **S** (Stache Passions), **P** (Pursonals), or **H** (Horyou).

This site would be good for someone who . . .

1. has a strong interest in personal appearance. ______
2. is hoping to adopt a new pet. ______
3. wants to watch a bit of light entertainment. ______
4. wants ideas for improving others' lives. ______
5. is interested in styles from the past. ______
6. wants to raise money for a charity. ______

C Find the words in the article that mean the following.

1. enough for a purpose ______________________
2. places where a discussion can take place ______________________
3. to like and be grateful for something ______________________
4. people who want to accomplish political or social change ______________________
5. plans of action ______________________

D **PAIR WORK** Do you belong to any specialized social networking sites? If yes, what is the focus? If not, what type of specialized site might you join?

2 Working 9 to 5

- Discuss opinions, advantages, and disadvantages of jobs
- Compare various jobs

1 SNAPSHOT

What do you want from your career?

☐ **Security**

If you want to have stability, choose a job that you can keep for your whole life. You could be a federal judge, a public school teacher, or a university professor.

☐ **Adventure**

Perhaps you can't picture yourself doing the same thing, at the same place, for years and years. In that case, be something that will allow you to explore other places and other cultures, like an environmentalist or a tour guide.

☐ **Money**

Do you want to have a high-paying job? You may want to look into being a financial analyst, a doctor, or a stockbroker.

Rank the factors from 1 (most important) to 3 (least important). Compare with a partner.
Which factors did you consider when you chose your present job or your future career? Why?

2 PERSPECTIVES Career choices

A Listen to students discuss career choices. Do you agree or disagree? Check (✓) the speaker you agree with more.

☐ I'd like to work in the video game industry. Playing games all day would be lots of fun.

☐ I disagree! Playing the same game every day for months would be boring.

☐ Designing clothes is not a man's job. Women are much more fascinated by fashion.

☐ Being a flight attendant sounds very exciting. Traveling all the time would be really interesting.

☐ But flight attendants get tired of traveling. They spend most of their time in airports!

☐ That's not true! Many great fashion designers are men. Just look at Michael Kors!

☐ I'd enjoy working with animals. I think working as a veterinarian could be rewarding.

☐ I'm not so sure. Animals can be very unpredictable. Getting a dog bite would be scary!

B Compare your responses with your classmates. Give more reasons to support your opinions.

3 GRAMMAR FOCUS

Gerund phrases

Gerund phrases as subjects	Gerund phrases as objects
Playing games all day would be lots of fun.	She'd be good at **testing games**.
Being a flight attendant sounds exciting.	He'd love **being a flight attendant**.
Designing clothes is not a man's job.	He wouldn't like **being a fashion designer**.
Working as a veterinarian could be rewarding.	She'd enjoy **working with animals**.

GRAMMAR PLUS see page 133

A Look at the gerund phrases in column A. Write your opinion of each job by choosing information from columns B and C. Then add two more gerund phrases and write similar sentences.

	A	B	C
1.	working from home	seems	awful
2.	doing volunteer work	could be	stressful
3.	having your own business	would be	fantastic
4.	working on a movie set	must be	fascinating
5.	being a teacher	wouldn't be	pretty difficult
6.	making a living as a tour guide	doesn't sound	kind of boring
7.	taking care of sick people		really rewarding
8.	retiring at age 40		very challenging
9.	______________________		
10.	______________________		

1. *Working from home could be very challenging.*

B **PAIR WORK** Give reasons for your opinions about the jobs in part A.

A: In my opinion, working from home could be very challenging.
B: Really? Why is that?
A: Because you have to learn to manage your time. It's easy to get distracted.
B: I'm not sure that's true. For me, working from home would be . . .

C **GROUP WORK** Complete the sentences with gerund phrases. Then take turns reading your sentences. Share the three most interesting sentences with the class.

1. I'd get tired of . . .
2. I'd be interested in . . .
3. I'd be very excited about . . .
4. I'd enjoy . . .
5. I think I'd be good at . . .
6. I wouldn't be very good at . . .

"I'd get tired of doing the same thing every day."

4 WORD POWER Suffixes

A Add the suffixes *-er, -or, -ist,* or *-ian* to form the names of these jobs. Write the words in the chart and add one more example to each column.

software develop *er*	freelance journal____	marketing direct____	politic____
computer technic____	guidance counsel____	project manag____	psychiatr____

-er	-or	-ist	-ian
software developer			

B **PAIR WORK** Can you give a definition for each job?

"A software developer is someone who creates apps for computers and other devices."

5 SPEAKING Career paths

GROUP WORK Talk about a career you would like to have. Use information from Exercises 1–4 or your own ideas. Other students ask follow-up questions.

A: I'd enjoy working as a guidance counselor.
B: Why is that?
A: Helping kids must be really rewarding.
C: Where would you work?
A: Well, I think I'd like to work at a high school. I enjoy working with teens.

6 WRITING What's more satisfying?

A **GROUP WORK** What would you choose: a job that you love that doesn't pay well, or a high-paying job that you don't like? Discuss and list the consequences of the two alternatives.

B Use the list to write a paragraph justifying your choice.

Having a high-paying job that you don't like could be very frustrating. First of all, you'd have to do something you don't like every day. You would have a lot of money. However, it's not worth it if . . .

useful expressions

First of all, . . .
In addition, . . .
Furthermore, . . .
For example, . . .
However, . . .
On the other hand, . . .
In conclusion, . . .

C **PAIR WORK** Read your partner's paragraph. Do you agree or disagree? Why or why not?

7 CONVERSATION It doesn't pay as much.

A Listen and practice.

Tyler: Guess what? . . . I've found a summer job!
Emma: That's great! Anything interesting?
Tyler: Yes, working at a beach resort.
Emma: Wow, that sounds fantastic!
Tyler: So, have *you* found anything?
Emma: Nothing yet, but I have a couple of leads. One is working as an intern for a news website – mostly answering emails and posts from readers. Or I can get a job as a camp counselor again.
Tyler: Being an intern sounds more challenging than working at a summer camp. You could earn college credits, and it's probably not as much work.
Emma: Yeah, but the internship doesn't pay as much as the summer camp job. Do they have another opening at the beach resort? That's the kind of job I'd really enjoy.

B Listen to the rest of the conversation. What is Tyler going to do at the resort?

8 GRAMMAR FOCUS

Comparisons

with adjectives	**with verbs**
. . . sounds **more/less** challenging **than** . . .	. . . earns **more/less than** . . .
. . . is hard**er than** . . .	. . . earns **as much as** . . .
. . . is **not as** hard **as** . . .	. . . does**n't** pay **as much as** . . .
with nouns	**with past participles**
. . . has **better/worse** hours **than** . . .	. . . is **better** paid **than** . . .
. . . has **more** education **than** . . .	. . . is **as** well paid **as** . . .
. . . is**n't as much** work **as** . . .	. . . is**n't as** well paid **as** . . .

GRAMMAR PLUS *see page 133*

A Complete the sentences using the words in parentheses. Compare with a partner. (More than one answer is possible.)

1. In my opinion, being a firefighter is ___________ (stressful) being a sales associate. In addition, sales associates have ___________ (hours) firefighters.
2. In general, doctors need ___________ (training) nutritionists. However, they usually ___________ (earn) nutritionists.
3. Game testers don't need ___________ (experience) software developers. As a result, they ___________ (earn) software developers.
4. A career in banking is often ___________ (demanding) a career in sales, but it is also ___________ (paid).

B **PAIR WORK** Compare the jobs in part A. Which would you choose? Why?

9 PRONUNCIATION Stress with compound nouns

A Listen and practice. Notice that the first word in these compound nouns has more stress. Then add two more compound nouns to the chart.

●	●	●	●
firefighter	game tester	guidance counselor	
hairstylist	flight attendant	project manager	

B **GROUP WORK** Which job in each column would be more challenging? Why? Tell the group. Pay attention to stress.

10 LISTENING It's not what I thought.

A Listen to Caden talk to Janelle about his job as a video game tester. Which parts of the job does he like and dislike? Check (✓) Like or Dislike.

		Like	Dislike
1.	The pay	☐	☐
2.	The hours	☐	☐
3.	Testing games	☐	☐
4.	Playing video games at home	☐	☐
5.	Thinking of new ideas for games	☐	☐

B Listen again. What does Caden decide to do?

C **PAIR WORK** What other advice would you give Caden?

11 DISCUSSION Which job would you take?

A What is a job you would like to have? What is a job you wouldn't like to have? Write each one on a separate slip of paper.

kindergarten teacher *tour guide*

B **GROUP WORK** Mix all the slips from your group. One student picks two slips and the group helps him or her decide between the two jobs.

A: You should take the job as a kindergarten teacher because you enjoy working with kids.

B: But being a tour guide sounds more exciting. I could travel more and earn more money.

C: But you'd work longer hours and . . .

12 INTERCHANGE 2 Networking

Would you be a good party planner? Go to Interchange 2 on page 115.

13 READING

A Skim the web posts. Which person works in the most traditional workplace? the least traditional?

THE PERFECT WORKPLACE?

What is your workplace like? Tell us and see how other places compare!

My workplace is cooler than any office I've ever seen. Working here is really stimulating. I share a table with my co-workers, and the workplace is flooded with light. Getting free meals is great, and there are relaxing activities like billiards and board games. Plus we get a membership to a local gym! It isn't all play, of course – we work very hard – but the perks make it better than any other job I can imagine.
Lauren L., *Palo Alto, California*

When I got my job as a project manager for a finance company in London, I imagined a modern building with views of the city and open workspaces. When I arrived for my first day, I was pretty surprised. I found a typical cubicle farm, with desks as far as the eye could see. It works for me, though. I can concentrate in my own space and then talk with colleagues in the meeting rooms. We do have a great gym on the ground floor, so that's a bonus!
Catherine D., *London, UK*

I work in a research laboratory at a botanical garden. Working in a lab isn't as tedious as it sounds. That's because a lot of my work takes place in the greenhouses or outdoors. I love spending time among plants, and I enjoy working with other scientists who share my interests. True, the workplace isn't very luxurious. We have a tiny break room that some people complain about, and there isn't a place to work out or anything, but being outdoors so much makes up for the disadvantages.
Mark T., *Bronx, New York*

B Read the web posts. Who would have written these sentences about their workplace? Write the names.

1. Working in different environments keeps me from getting bored. ________
2. It's a perfect environment for sharing new ideas with co-workers. ________
3. There's nothing unique about it, but it's fine for the kind of work we do. ________
4. Visitors might get the idea that we don't take our work seriously. ________
5. Some employees are dissatisfied with the workplace, but I don't mind it. ________
6. I love being able to exercise without leaving the building. ________

C Find the words below in the web posts. Then complete the sentences with the words.

stimulating perk cubicle tedious luxurious

1. One ________ of my job is that we get free tickets to cultural and sporting events.
2. Working with creative people is very ________ because we can share lots of great ideas!
3. The disadvantage of working in a ________ is that you can hear everything that's going on around you.
4. The marketing director's office is very ________, with beautiful furniture and valuable paintings.
5. Working with numbers all day seems ________ to some people, but I enjoy it.

D **PAIR WORK** Which of the workplaces would you like the best? What features of a workplace matter most to you?

Units 1–2 Progress check

SELF-ASSESSMENT

How well can you do these things? Check (✓) the boxes.

I can . . .	Very well	OK	A little
Describe personalities (Ex. 1)	☐	☐	☐
Ask about and express preferences (Ex. 1)	☐	☐	☐
Understand and express complaints (Ex. 2)	☐	☐	☐
Give opinions about jobs (Ex. 3)	☐	☐	☐
Describe and compare different jobs (Ex. 4)	☐	☐	☐

1 SPEAKING Doing things together

A What two qualities would you like someone to have for these situations?

A person to . . .

1. be your business partner __________ __________
2. share an apartment with __________ __________
3. go on vacation with __________ __________
4. work on a class project with __________ __________

B CLASS ACTIVITY Find someone you could do each thing with.

A: What kind of person would you like to be your business partner?
B: I'd choose someone who has initiative and is hardworking.
A: Me, too! And I'd like someone who I can . . .

2 LISTENING I know what you mean!

A Listen to Suki and Andy discuss these topics. Complete the chart.

	Andy's biggest complaint	Suki's biggest complaint
1. websites		
2. children		
3. taxi drivers		
4. restaurant servers		

B PAIR WORK What is your biggest complaint about any of the topics in part A?

"I hate it when you can't find the products you want on a company's website."

3 SURVEY Job evaluation

A GROUP WORK What job would you like to have? Ask and answer questions in groups to complete the chart.

	Name	Job	Good points	Bad points
1.				
2.				
3.				
4.				

A: What job would you like to have?
B: I'd like to be a flight attendant.
C: What would be the good points?
B: Well, traveling around the world would be exciting.
D: Would there be any bad points?
B: Oh, sure. I'd dislike packing and unpacking all the time. . . .

useful expressions

I would(n't) be good at . . .
I would enjoy/dislike . . .
I would(n't) be interested in . . .
I would(n't) be excited about . . .

B GROUP WORK Who thought of the most unusual job? the best job? the worst job?

4 ROLE PLAY Choosing a job

Student A: Your partner, Student B, is looking for a job. Based on his or her opinions about jobs in Exercise 3, suggest two other jobs that Student B might enjoy.

Student B: You are looking for a job. Student A suggests two jobs for you. Discuss the questions below. Then choose one of the jobs.

Which one is more interesting? harder?
Which one has better hours? better pay?
Which job would you rather have?

A: I thought of two other jobs for you. You could be a hairstylist or a truck driver.
B: Hmm. Which job has better hours?
A: Well, a hairstylist has better hours, but it's not as . . .

Change roles and try the role play again.

WHAT'S NEXT?

Look at your Self-assessment again. Do you need to review anything?

3 Lend a hand.

- Discuss favors, borrowing, and lending
- Leave messages with requests

1 SNAPSHOT

ANNOYING FAVORS PEOPLE ASK

Could you . . .

1. babysit my kids on the weekend?
2. watch my stuff for a few minutes?
3. let me use your credit card?
4. drive me to the airport?
5. let me use your passcode to download a movie?
6. help me move to my new apartment?
7. come with me to my niece's school concert?
8. let me stay at your place for a couple of weeks?
9. donate to my favorite charity?
10. co-sign a bank loan for me?

Imagine that a close friend asked you each of these favors. Which would you agree to do? What are three other favors that you dislike being asked?

2 CONVERSATION Thanks a million.

A Listen and practice.

Carlos: Hey, Keiko. What's up?
Keiko: Hi, Carlos. I was wondering if you could help me. I'm moving to my new apartment this weekend, and my car is pretty small. Can I borrow your truck, please?
Carlos: Um, I need it on Saturday, but you can borrow it on Sunday.
Keiko: Thanks so much.
Carlos: Sure. So, have you packed already?
Keiko: Uh-huh. I mean, I'll have everything packed by Sunday. You know, I think some of my boxes are going to be kind of heavy. Would you mind helping me put them in your truck on Sunday?
Carlos: I guess not. I suppose you want my help taking them out of the truck, too?
Keiko: Oh, that'd be great. Thanks a million, Carlos!

B Listen to two more calls Keiko makes. What else does she need help with? Do her friends agree to help?

3 GRAMMAR FOCUS

Requests with modals, *if* clauses, and gerunds

Less formal	**Can I** borrow your truck, please?
	Could you lend me your truck, please?
	Is it OK if I use your credit card?
	Do you mind if I use your credit card?
	Would it be all right if I **used** your credit card?
	Would you mind if I borrow**ed** your truck?
	Would you mind help**ing** me on Sunday?
More formal	**I was wondering if** you **could** help me move.

GRAMMAR PLUS *see page 134*

A Circle the correct answers. Then practice with a partner.

1. **A:** **Is it OK if** / **Would** / **Do you mind** I use your cell phone? Mine just died.
   B: No problem, but can you keep it short? I'm expecting an important phone call.
2. **A:** Would you mind if I **stay** / **staying** / **stayed** at your place for the weekend?
   B: Not at all. It'll be fun to have you stay with us.
3. **A:** I was wondering **I could** / **if I could** / **if I would** borrow your car tomorrow.
   B: Sure, that's fine. Just be careful. I've only had it for a couple of months.
4. **A:** Could you **lend** / **lending** / **lent** me $20?
   B: I'm sorry. I don't have any money to spare right now.
5. **A:** Would you mind **help** / **helped** / **helping** me pack my stuff this weekend?
   B: No, I don't mind. I'm not doing anything then.
6. **A:** **Would you mind** / **Can** / **Is it OK if** you feed my cats while I'm on vacation, please?
   B: Sorry, I don't get along with cats.

B Rewrite these sentences to make them more formal requests. Then practice making your requests with a partner. Accept or decline each request.

1. Come to my cousin's wedding with me.
2. Can I borrow your notes to study for the test?
3. Can you lend me your camera to take with me on my vacation?
4. Drive me to the airport.
5. Help me paint my apartment.
6. I'd like to borrow your cell phone to call a friend in London.

1. *Would you mind coming to my cousin's wedding with me?*

4 PRONUNCIATION Unreleased consonants

A Listen and practice. Notice that when /t/, /d/, /k/, /g/, /p/, and /b/ are followed by other consonant sounds, they are unreleased.

Coul**d** Crai**g** ta**ke** care of my pe**t** skunk?
Can you as**k** Bo**b** to hel**p** me?

B Circle the unreleased consonants in the conversations. Listen and check. Then practice the conversations with a partner.

1. **A:** I was wondering if I could borrow that book.
   B: Yes, but can you take it back to Doug tomorrow?
2. **A:** Would you mind giving Albert some help moving that big bed?
   B: Sorry, but my doctor said my back needs rest.

5 LISTENING I was wondering . . .

A Listen to three telephone conversations. Write down what each caller requests. Does the other person agree to the request? Check (✓) Yes or No.

	Request	Yes	No
1. Jesse		☐	☐
2. Liz		☐	☐
3. Min-jun		☐	☐

B **PAIR WORK** Use the chart to act out each conversation in your own words.

6 WRITING A message with requests

A Write a message to a classmate asking for several favors. Explain why you need help.

B **PAIR WORK** Exchange messages. Write a reply accepting or declining the requests.

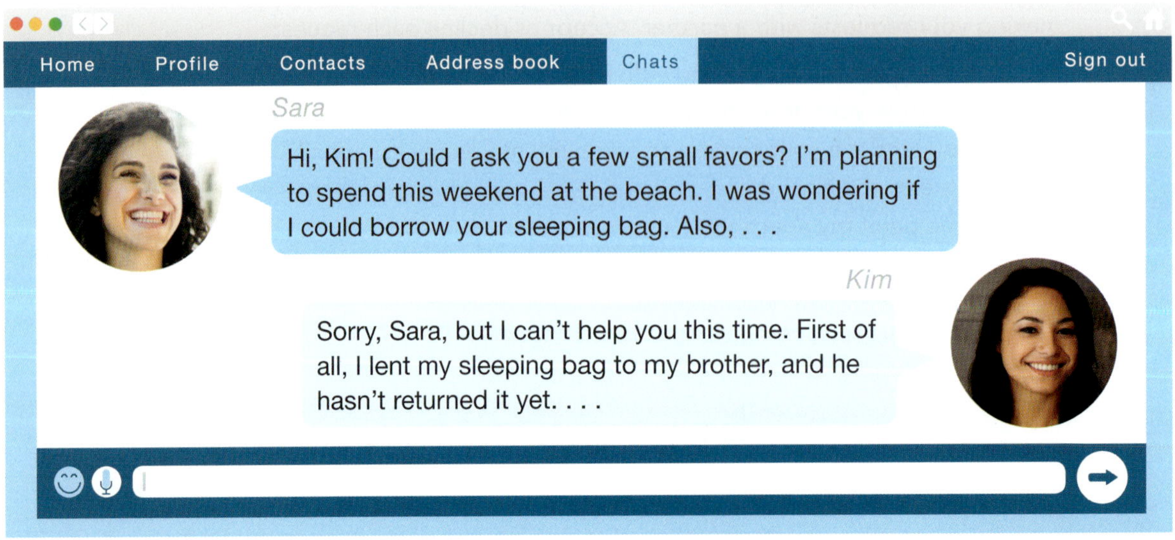

7 INTERCHANGE 3 Beg and borrow

Find out how generous you are. Go to Interchange 3 on page 116.

8 WORD POWER Verb-noun collocations

A Which verb is not usually paired with each noun? Put a line through the verb. Then compare with a partner.

1. return / do / ask for / ~~make~~ — a favor
2. owe / offer / do / accept — an apology
3. receive / accept / turn down / offer — an invitation
4. do / receive / give / accept — a gift
5. do / return / make / receive — a phone call
6. accept / make / decline / offer — a request
7. receive / return / do / give — a compliment

B **PAIR WORK** Add two questions to the list using the collocations in part A. Then take turns asking and answering the questions.

1. What are nice ways to return a favor? How do you usually return favors?
2. Have you ever invented an excuse to turn down an invitation? What excuse did you give?
3. When was the last time you declined a request? What was the request?
4. ______________________________
5. ______________________________

9 PERSPECTIVES Can you tell her . . . ?

A Listen to the requests people make at the school where Mary Martin teaches. Complete each request with *ask* or *tell*.

1. If you see Mary, can you ______ her that she left her phone in my car?
2. If you see Mary, could you ______ her whether or not she is coming to the teachers' meeting?
3. If you see Ms. Martin, can you ______ her if she's graded our tests yet?
4. If you see Mary, please ______ her not to forget the students' reports.
5. If you see Mary, could you ______ her to find me in the cafeteria after her meeting?
6. If you see Ms. Martin, would you ______ her what time I can talk to her about my homework?

B Who do you think made each request? the school coordinator? another teacher? a student?

10 GRAMMAR FOCUS

Indirect requests

Statements		**Indirect requests introduced by *that***
Mary, you left your phone in my car.	→	Could you tell Mary (**that**) **she left her phone in my car**?
Imperatives		**Indirect requests using infinitives**
Mary, don't forget the students' reports.	→	Can you tell Mary **not to forget the students' reports**?
Yes/No questions		**Indirect requests introduced by *if* or *whether***
Ms. Martin, have you graded our tests?	→	Can you ask her **if she's graded our tests yet**?
Mary, are you coming to the meeting?	→	Could you ask her **whether or not she is coming to the meeting**?
Wh-questions		**Indirect requests introduced by a question word**
Mary, where are you having lunch?	→	Can you ask Mary **where she's having lunch**?
Ms. Martin, what time can I talk to you about my homework?	→	Would you ask her **what time I can talk to her about my homework**?

GRAMMAR PLUS *see page 134*

Read the things people want to say to Mary. Rewrite the sentences as indirect requests. Then compare with a partner.

1. Mary, did you get my message about your phone?
2. Mary, will you give me a ride to school tomorrow?
3. Ms. Martin, when is our assignment due?
4. Mary, why didn't you meet us at the cafeteria for lunch?
5. Ms. Martin, I won't be in class tomorrow night.
6. Mary, are you going to the school party on Saturday?
7. Mary, please return my call when you get your phone back.
8. Mary, have you received my wedding invitation?

1. *Could you ask Mary if she got my message about her phone?*

11 SPEAKING No problem.

A Write five requests for your partner to pass on to classmates.

Would you ask Keith if he can turn off his phone in class?

B **CLASS ACTIVITY** Ask your partner to pass on your requests. Go around the class and make your partner's requests. Then tell your partner how people responded.

A: Would you ask Keith if he can turn off his phone in class?
B: No problem. . . . Keith, could you turn off your cell phone in class?
C: I'm sorry, but I can't! I'm expecting an important phone call.
B: Lee, Keith says he's expecting an important phone call.

12 READING

A Scan the article. What are the three problems?

HOME NEWS ARTICLES COMMUNITY

CAN YOU TELL IT LIKE IT IS?

There are some things that are almost impossible to say to our close friends – especially if we want them to be our friends for life. Are you wondering what problems others have with bringing up difficult subjects? Read on.

1. "I can't stand your other friends."

My best friend sometimes hangs out with some people that I really don't like. I think they have a bad influence on her, and she only spends time with them because they are "cool." Could you tell me if I should bring the matter up with her, or if it would be better for me to keep quiet? I don't want to lose her as a friend. – Carly

2. "I won't help you cheat."

My closest friend has lost interest in school and studying. He says he's bored with the whole thing, so he often asks me whether I'll do him a favor and let him copy my homework. So far I've said no, but he keeps asking me. I told him that I think we'll get in trouble, but he just laughed and told me not to worry. I don't want to put my grades at risk, but I'm afraid to confront my friend about this, so I just keep avoiding the topic. How can I get him to stop asking? I was wondering if you could give me some tips for handling my problem. – Matt

3. "No, I CAN'T do that for you!"

My best friend and I get along really well, but she is constantly asking me to do things for her. "Could you help me pick out some new clothes? Would you mind if I borrowed your car? Can you look after my apartment while I'm away?" And these are just a few examples. I've said yes so many times that now I'm afraid I'll hurt her feelings if I say no. Any ideas? – Dana

B Read the article. Then answer the questions.

1. Why is Carly concerned about her friend? ____________________

2. What is Matt most worried about? ____________________

3. Why is Dana afraid to say no to her friend? ____________________

4. Who is this advice best for?

a. Say that you know your friend can handle the work himself. __________

b. Agree to some requests, but only if your friend does something in return. __________

c. Tell your friend there are more important things than being popular. __________

C What do the underlined words in the article refer to? Write the correct word(s).

1. them __________

2. the matter __________

3. the whole thing __________

4. this __________

5. these __________

D **PAIR WORK** Have you ever had similar problems with friends? How were the problems resolved? What advice would you give to Carly, Matt, and Dana?

4 What happened?

- Describe past events
- Tell stories

1 SNAPSHOT

NEWS
Several Streets Closed After "Suspicious Package" Was Found

HEALTH
Why Weight Loss Isn't the Same as Being Healthy

TRENDING TOPICS
The Earth Is Getting Warmer and the Signs Are Everywhere

ARTS
The Top-Rated TV Shows You Need to Be Watching Right Now

SCIENCE
Women Need More Sleep Than Men Because They Use More of Their Brains

TECH
Here Are the Five Must-Have Apps for Runners

Which story would you like to read? Why?
What types of stories do you usually read online?
Where do you get your news? What's happening in the news today?

2 PERSPECTIVES Listen up.

A Listen to what people are listening to on their way to work. Which stories from Exercise 1 are they related to?

Hey, I just downloaded this incredible app. I used it this morning and I think you're going to love it. While I was working out, it calculated exactly how many calories I burned. The bad thing is, it tells me I still need to run about 4 miles to burn off last night's dinner.

As scientists were doing some research on the effects of sleep deprivation, they discovered that women need about 20 more minutes of sleep a night than men do. They think the reason is that women tend to do several tasks at once, which makes their brains work harder.

Hi, Jeff. We're canceling our meeting in the downtown office this morning. We just learned that the police have closed all the streets in the area. It seems that a man was looking for his lost cat when he found a suspicious package inside a trash can. In the end, it was just an old box of chocolates.

B Which is a message from a co-worker? a message from a friend? a podcast?

3 GRAMMAR FOCUS

Past continuous vs. simple past

Use the past continuous for an ongoing action in the past.
Use the simple past for an event that interrupts that action.

Past continuous	*Simple past*
While I **was working** out,	it **calculated** how many calories I burned.
As scientists **were doing** research,	they **discovered** that women need more sleep than men.
A man **was looking** for his cat	when he **found** a suspicious package inside a trash can.

GRAMMAR PLUS *see page 135*

A Complete the stories using the past continuous or simple past forms of the verbs. Then compare with a partner.

1. **Bad memory, bad luck:** Marcia Murphy ________________ (donate) her old pants to a thrift shop. As she ________________ (walk) home, she ________________ (remember) she ________________ (leave) $20 in her pants pocket.
2. **Good intentions, bad interpretation:** Jason Clark ________________ (walk) home one day, when he ________________ (see) a little puppy crying on the sidewalk, so he ________________ (stop) to help. As he ________________ (pick) him up, a woman ________________ (come) from nowhere screaming: "Stop that guy. He's trying to steal my puppy." Jason ________________ (end) up spending three hours at the police station.
3. **A bad ride, a bad fall:** On her birthday last year, Diane Larson ________________ (drive) to work when she ________________ (have) a bad accident. This year, just to be safe, she decided to stay home on her birthday. Unfortunately, that night while she ________________ (sleep) in her apartment, the floor of her living room ________________ (collapse) and she ________________ (fall) into her neighbor's apartment.

B **GROUP WORK** Take turns retelling the stories in part A. Add your own ideas and details to make the stories more interesting!

4 PRONUNCIATION Intonation in complex sentences

A Listen and practice. Notice how each clause in a complex sentence has its own intonation pattern.

As Marcia was walking home, she remembered she left $20 in her pants pocket.

A man was looking for his cat when he found a package.

B **PAIR WORK** Use your imagination to make complex sentences. Take turns starting and finishing the sentences. Pay attention to intonation.

A: As Lee was coming to school today . . .
B: . . . he saw a parade coming down the street.

5 LISTENING Crazy but true!

A Listen to three news stories. Number the pictures from 1 to 3. (There is one extra picture.)

B Listen again. Take notes on each story.

	Where did it happen?	When did it happen?	What happened?
1.			
2.			
3.			

6 WRITING A personal account

A Think of a story that happened to you or to someone you know. Choose one of the titles below, or create your own.

A Scary Experience
I'll Never Forget That Day
I Was Really Lucky
I Can't Believe It Happened

B Write your story. First, answer these questions.

Who was involved?
Where did it happen?
When did it happen?
What happened?

I Was Really Lucky

Last year, I took a trip to see my grandparents. I was waiting in the airport for my flight when a storm hit, and all the flights were cancelled. Luckily, I . . .

C **GROUP WORK** Take turns telling your stories. Other students ask questions. Who has the best story?

7 CONVERSATION That's terrible!

A Listen and practice.

CAROL Guess what? Someone stole my new bike yesterday!

MILO Oh, no! What happened?

CAROL Well, I was having lunch with a friend, and I had parked it on the street, just like I always do. When I came back, someone had stolen it. I guess I'd forgotten to lock it up.

MILO That's terrible! Did you report the theft to the police?

CAROL Yes, I did. And I also listed it on that site for stolen and lost bikes. But I doubt I'll ever get it back.

B Listen to the rest of the conversation. What did Milo have stolen once? Where was he?

8 GRAMMAR FOCUS

Past perfect

Use the past perfect for an event that occurred before another event in the past.

Past event	Past perfect event
I **was having** lunch with a friend,	and I **had parked** my bike on the street.
When I **came back,**	someone **had stolen** it.
They **were able** to steal it	because I **had forgotten** to lock it up.

GRAMMAR PLUS *see page 135*

A Write the correct verbs to complete the sentences. Then compare with a partner.

1. I ________________ (took/had taken) a trip to London last year. I was a bit scared because I ________________ (didn't travel/hadn't traveled) abroad before, but everything was perfect.
2. I ________________ (visited/was visiting) the British Museum one afternoon when I ________________ (ran/had run) into an old school friend who I ________________ (didn't see/hadn't seen) for over 10 years.
3. One weekend, we ________________ (were driving/had driven) to Liverpool when we ________________ (ran/were running) out of gas on the highway because we ________________ (forgot/had forgotten) to fill up the tank before leaving. Fortunately, a truck driver ________________ (stopped/had stopped) and ________________ (helped/had helped) us.
4. On the last day, as I ________________ (was going/had gone) up to my hotel room, I ________________ (got/had gotten) stuck in the elevator. After I ________________ (was/had been) stuck for an hour, someone ________________ (started/had started) it again.

B **PAIR WORK** Complete the sentences with your own ideas.

Until last year, I had never . . .
One day, as I was . . .

9 WORD POWER Exceptional events

A Match the words in column A with the definitions in column B.

A	B
1. coincidence ______	**a.** an unexpected event that brings good fortune
2. dilemma ______	**b.** a situation that involves a difficult choice
3. disaster ______	**c.** something puzzling or unexplained
4. emergency ______	**d.** an event that causes suffering or destruction
5. lucky break ______	**e.** a great success or achievement
6. mishap ______	**f.** an accident, mistake, or unlucky event
7. mystery ______	**g.** a sudden, dangerous situation that requires quick action
8. triumph ______	**h.** a situation when two similar things happen at the same time for no reason

B **PAIR WORK** Choose one kind of event from part A. Write a situation for it.

> A man bought an old house for $10,000. As he was cleaning the attic of his new home, he found an old painting by a famous painter. He had never collected art, but when he took it to a museum, he found out it was worth almost one million dollars. (lucky break)

C **GROUP WORK** Read your situation. Can others guess which kind of event it describes?

10 SPEAKING It's a story about . . .

GROUP WORK Have you ever experienced the events in Exercise 9, part A? Tell your group about it. Answer any questions.

A: It's a story about a coincidence.
B: What happened?
A: My sister bought a new dress for her graduation party. She had saved for months to buy it. When she got to the party, another girl was wearing the exact same dress!
C: Wow! That's more than a coincidence. It's a disaster! And what did she do?

11 INTERCHANGE 4 Spin a yarn

Tell a story. Go to Interchange 4 on page 117.

12 READING

A Skim the article. Was the story about lice true or false?

Menu Articles Community Search Sign in / Sign up

Believing More Than We Should

Is everything you read on the Internet true? If your answer is "no," you are absolutely right. Many stories and even photos are not to be trusted. And don't believe that because a good friend or a well-known news source has posted something that it is necessarily trustworthy.

There are many reasons for the spread of inaccurate content on the Internet. One reason is that satirical websites can create very believable stories, which they invent in order to make a point or to make people laugh. Other reasons might be an attempt to gain more readers, a desire to damage someone's reputation, or simple curiosity about how far a fake story can spread.

One story that spread throughout the media before anyone had checked the facts involved teenagers, selfies, and head lice. The article claimed that when teenagers were posing together for selfies, their heads often touched and the tiny insects were jumping from head to head. The article went on to say that this was causing a massive outbreak of lice. Some major websites and news outlets picked up the story, not even bothering to consult the experts. It turned out that some entrepreneurs who were marketing a new treatment for head lice had made up the story and posted it. Their motivation was to get attention and more business.

The spread of this story is understandable. It involved one epidemic (selfies) causing another (lice), and the "ick" factor was irresistible. Because there is so much false information online, there are now websites, such as *Snopes* and *Factcheck*, which exist specifically to find out if stories are true or not. So the next time you see a story that sounds too good to be true, at least you have somewhere to turn for verification before you spread false information to all your friends.

B Read the article. Find the words in italics in the article. Then check (✓) the meaning of each word.

1. *inaccurate*	☐ not exact or true	☐ shocking or disgusting
2. *satirical*	☐ humorously critical	☐ completely factual
3. *reputation*	☐ hurtful news about someone	☐ public opinion of someone
4. *massive*	☐ small	☐ very large
5. *irresistible*	☐ hard to prove	☐ hard to fight against
6. *verification*	☐ proof of truth	☐ another opinion

C **PAIR WORK** Discuss these questions.

Do you think you would have believed the story about selfies and head lice?
Do you think the creation of the story was justified or not?
Who do you think is most responsible for the story being so popular?
Do you think there should be a penalty for spreading false information? If so, what should it be?

D **GROUP WORK** Have you ever read a story that turned out to be false? How did you find out the truth?

Units 3–4 Progress check

SELF-ASSESSMENT

How well can you do these things? Check (✓) the boxes.

I can . . .	Very well	OK	A little
Discuss favors (Ex. 1)	☐	☐	☐
Leave messages with requests (Ex. 2)	☐	☐	☐
Tell a story, making clear the sequence of events (Ex. 3, 5)	☐	☐	☐
Understand the sequence of events in a story (Ex. 4)	☐	☐	☐

1 ROLE PLAY Save the date!

Student A: You are planning a class party at your house. Think of three things you need help with. Then call a classmate and ask for help.

Student B: Student A is planning a party. Agree to help with some things, but not everything.

"Hi, Martina. I'm calling about the party. Would you mind . . . ?"

Change roles and try the role play again.

2 DISCUSSION Who said it?

A GROUP WORK Take turns reading each request. Then discuss the questions and come up with possible answers.

Tell Rita that I'm going to be a half hour late for our meeting. Ask her to wait for me in her office.

Tell your officers that he's white and wears a blue collar with his name on it – Rex. Please call if you find him.

I'm sorry to bother you, but I really need it back for the office party on Friday. Please ask Sue to bring it over before that.

1. What is the situation?
2. Who is the request for? Who do you think received the request and passed it on?
3. Give an indirect request for each situation.

"Could you tell Rita . . . ?"

B CLASS ACTIVITY Compare your answers. Which group has the most interesting answers for each message?

3 SPEAKING And then . . . ?

A PAIR WORK Choose a type of event from the box. Then make up a title for a story about it. Write the title on a piece of paper.

disaster **emergency** **lucky break** **mystery** **triumph**

B PAIR WORK Exchange titles with another pair. Discuss the questions *who, what, where, when, why,* and *how* about the other pair's title. Then make up a story.

C Share your story with the pair who wrote the title.

The Mystery of the Message in a Bottle

I was walking on the beach when I saw a bottle with a message inside. The bottle looked very old, and it was hard to open it. Inside there was a message: "My beloved Catherine, I hope you . . ."

4 LISTENING What happened first?

Listen to each situation. Number the events from 1 to 3.

1.	☐ She got sick.	☐ She went on vacation.	☐ She went back to work.
2.	☐ John called me.	☐ I didn't get the message.	☐ I changed phone numbers.
3.	☐ I was very nervous.	☐ I left the office.	☐ I felt relieved.
4.	☐ We went out.	☐ My cousin stopped by.	☐ I was watching a movie.

5 DISCUSSION Beginning, middle, and end

GROUP WORK Choose the beginning of a story from column A and an ending from column B. Discuss interesting or unusual events that could link A to B. Then make up a story.

A

Once, I . . .
accepted an interesting invitation.
was asked to do an unusual favor.
received an unexpected phone call.
owed someone a big apology.

B

Believe it or not, . . .
I got home, and there were 30 people in my living room!
I had no idea where I was.
when I got there, everyone had left.
it was the star of my favorite TV show!

A: Once, I accepted an interesting invitation.
B: Let's see. . . . I was biking home when I got a text from an old friend.
C: I hadn't seen him in over five years.
D: I was really surprised, but . . .

WHAT'S NEXT?

Look at your Self-assessment again. Do you need to review anything?

5 Expanding your horizons

▸ Discuss living in a foreign country
▸ Describe cultural expectations and differences

1 PERSPECTIVES Challenges of living abroad

A Listen to people talk about moving to a foreign country. Check (✓) the concerns you think you would share.

- ☐ "One thing that I'd really miss is hanging out with my friends." ______
- ☐ "Something that I'd be worried about is the local food. I'm a picky eater." ______
- ☐ "Getting used to a different culture might be difficult at first." ______
- ☐ "I'd be worried about not knowing how to get around in a new city." ______
- ☐ "The people that I'd miss the most are my parents. We're very close." ______
- ☐ "Not knowing the local customs is something I'd be concerned about." ______
- ☐ "I'd be nervous about getting sick and not knowing how to explain my symptoms." ______
- ☐ "Communicating in a foreign language could be a challenge." ______

B Rate each concern from 1 (not worried at all) to 5 (really worried). What would be your biggest concern? Why?

2 WORD POWER Mixed feelings

A These words are used to describe how people sometimes feel when they live in a foreign country. Which are positive (**P**)? Which are negative (**N**)? Write P or N.

anxious	______	embarrassed	______	insecure	______
comfortable	______	enthusiastic	______	nervous	______
confident	______	excited	______	uncertain	______
curious	______	fascinated	______	uncomfortable	______
depressed	______	homesick	______	worried	______

B **GROUP WORK** Tell your group about other situations in which you experienced the feelings in part A. What made you feel that way? How do you feel about the situations now?

A: I felt very embarrassed yesterday. I fell down the stairs in a restaurant.
B: How did it happen?
A: I think I slipped on something.
C: Did you get hurt?
A: Just a couple of bruises, but the restaurant manager was worried, so he convinced me to go to the hospital.

confident

3 GRAMMAR FOCUS

Noun phrases containing relative clauses

Something (that) I'd be worried about is the local food.

One thing (that) I'd really miss is hanging out with my friends.

The people (who/that) I'd miss the most are my parents.

The local food **is something (that) I'd be worried about.**

Hanging out with my friends is **one thing (that) I'd really miss**.

My parents are **the people (who/that) I'd miss the most.**

GRAMMAR PLUS *see page 136*

A Complete the sentences about living in a foreign country. Use the phrases below. Then compare with a partner.

my friends	trying new foods	being away from home	getting lost in a new city
my family	feeling like an outsider	my grandmother's cooking	not understanding people
getting sick	making new friends	speaking a foreign language	learning about a different culture

1. . . . is something I'd be very enthusiastic about.
2. The thing I'd probably be most excited about is . . .
3. . . . is something I'd really miss.
4. Two things I'd be homesick for are . . .
5. Something I'd get depressed about is . . .
6. . . . is one thing that I might be embarrassed about.
7. The thing I'd feel most uncomfortable about would be . . .
8. . . . are the people who I'd miss the most.
9. One thing I'd be insecure about is . . .
10. . . . are two things I'd be anxious about.

B Now complete three sentences in part A with your own information.

1. *Going to different festivals is something I'd be very enthusiastic about.*

C **GROUP WORK** Rewrite your sentences from part B in another way. Then compare. Do others feel the same way?

1. *I'd be very enthusiastic about going to different festivals.*

4 PRONUNCIATION Word stress in sentences

A Listen and practice. Notice that the important words in a sentence have more stress.

Uruguay is a country that I'd like to live in.

Speaking a foreign language is something I'd be anxious about.

Trying new foods is something I'd be curious about.

B **PAIR WORK** Mark the stress in the sentences you wrote in Exercise 3, part A. Then practice the sentences. Pay attention to word stress.

9 LISTENING Different cultures

A Listen to people describe customs they observed abroad. Complete the chart.

	Where was the person?	What was the custom?	How did the person react?
1. Carla			
2. Nate			
3. Shauna			

B **PAIR WORK** Which custom would you have the most trouble adapting to? Why?

10 SPEAKING Local customs

A **PAIR WORK** What should a visitor to your country know about local customs? Make a list. Include these points.

greeting and addressing someone
eating or drinking in public
taking photographs
giving gifts
dressing appropriately
visiting someone's home
using public transportation
tipping

When you ride in a cab, you're supposed to tip the driver.

B **GROUP WORK** Compare your lists with another pair. Then share experiences in which you (or someone you know) *didn't* follow the appropriate cultural behavior. What happened?

A: Once, when traveling abroad, I took a cab, and I didn't give the driver a tip.
B: What happened?
A: Well, he looked kind of angry. Then my friend gave the guy a tip, and I realized my mistake. It was a little embarrassing. . . .

11 WRITING A tourist pamphlet

A **GROUP WORK** Choose five points from the list you made in Exercise 10. Use them to write and design a pamphlet for tourists visiting your country or city.

WE HOPE YOU ENJOY YOUR STAY.

When you visit Italy, there are some important things you should know. For example, you can't buy a bus ticket on the bus in most big cities. Actually, you are supposed to . . .

B **CLASS ACTIVITY** Present your pamphlets. Which of the points were the most useful? What other information would a tourist need to know?

12 INTERCHANGE 5 Cultural dos and taboos

Compare customs in different countries. Go to Interchange 5 on page 118.

13 READING

A Scan the blog. What kinds of culture shock did the writer experience?

CULTURE SHOCK

PROFILE | PHOTOS | BLOG | COMMUNITY

I'm an exchange student from Spain navigating life in the United States. *Lucia M.*

JANUARY 15 ______________________

My hometown of Seville, Spain is a city with active, passionate people and a lively nightlife, so coming to Seattle, in the United States, has been quite an eye-opener. Americans think of Seattle as an exciting city, but the first time I went out with friends on a Saturday night, there was hardly anybody out in the streets. I actually thought something was wrong! Then my friend explained that most of their social life takes place indoors. In Seville, people fill the streets year-round, and Saturday nights are like a big celebration.

JANUARY 22 ______________________

After a couple of weeks of classes, I've begun to notice some differences between Spanish students and American students. In Spain, students talk a lot during class, and it's not always related to the lesson. On the other hand, when Spanish students are enthusiastic about a lesson, they often ask unusual questions, and it's common to stay after class to talk to the teacher. American students are expected to talk less and listen more, and many of them take detailed notes. Most of them leave the room as soon as the class ends, though, and are already focused on the next lesson.

FEBRUARY 8 ______________________

Before I came to the United States, a friend who had studied here told me that American friends don't greet each other like we do in Spain, where we touch cheeks and make kissing sounds. Americans often hug each other, but kissing is not common, and I've gotten used to that. So imagine my surprise when I was introduced to a new girl, and she immediately gave me the Spanish-style double kiss. When I asked my friend about this later, she explained that the girl was from a family of actors, and that "air-kissing" was a usual greeting for artistic people. My friend also said that some outgoing people greet their friends or family this way, but that it would make other people feel uncomfortable. I think I'll stick to handshakes and hugs while I'm here!

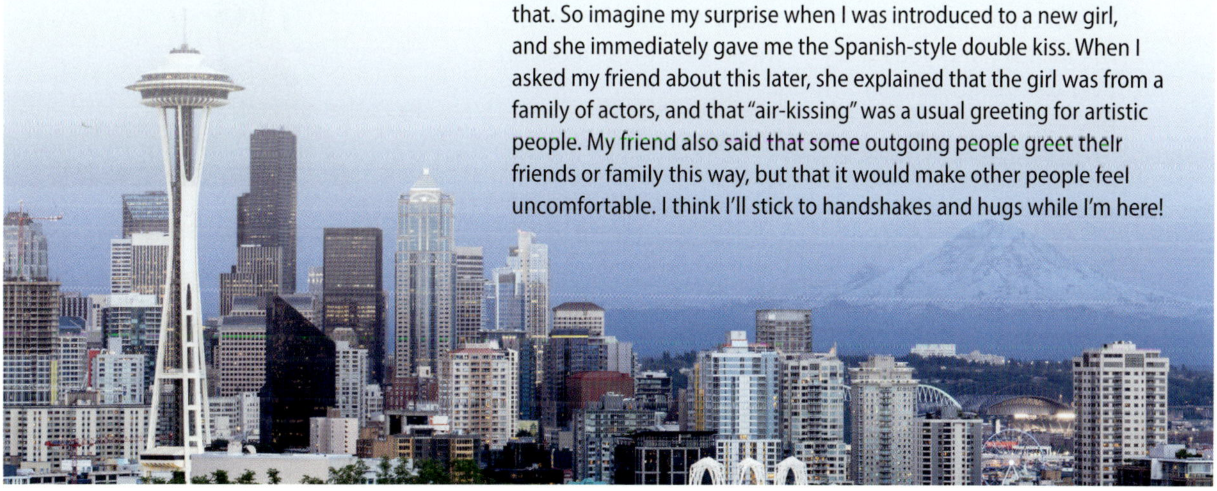

B Read the blog. Then add the correct title to each entry.

Meeting and greeting   Where's the party?   Class contrasts

C Check (✓) True or False for each statement. Then correct the false statements.

	True	False	
1. The writer was nervous because the Seattle streets were crowded at night.	☐	☐	
2. Spanish students often stay after class to ask questions.	☐	☐	
3. Hugging is a usual greeting among friends in Spain.	☐	☐	
4. The writer plans to change the way she greets American friends.	☐	☐	

D **PAIR WORK** How do things in your city compare with Seville? with Seattle?

6 That needs fixing.

- Describe problems and make complaints
- Discuss what needs fixing

1 SNAPSHOT

Some common complaints

Banking
The credit card company bills you for something you didn't buy.

Online shopping
The store sends you an incorrect size.

Internet providers
The Internet connection is not reliable, and you hardly ever get the speed you pay for.

Restaurants
The server rushes you to leave as soon as you finish your meal.

Vehicles
Your new car consumes too much gas.

Repair services
Your TV breaks again, a week after it was repaired.

Parking garage
Someone damages your car.

Have you ever had any of these problems? Which ones?
What would you do in each of these situations?
What other complaints have you had?

2 PERSPECTIVES That's not right!

A Listen to people describe complaints. Check (✓) what you think each person should do.

1. "I got a new suitcase, but when I arrived home, I noticed the lining was torn."
   - ☐ take it back to the store
   - ☐ ask the store to send you a new one
2. "My father sent me a coffee mug with my favorite team's logo, but when it arrived, it was chipped."
   - ☐ tell your father about it
   - ☐ contact the seller yourself
3. "I lent my ski pants to a friend, but when he returned them, there was a big stain on them."
   - ☐ clean them yourself
   - ☐ ask him to have them cleaned
4. "My boss borrowed my camera for a company event, and now the lens is scratched."
   - ☐ talk to him or her about it
   - ☐ say nothing and repair it yourself
5. "I bought a new washing machine just a month ago, and it's leaking already."
   - ☐ ask for a refund
   - ☐ send it back and get a new one

B Have you ever had similar complaints? What happened? What did you do?

3 GRAMMAR FOCUS

Describing problems 1

With past participles as adjectives	With nouns
The suitcase lining is **torn**.	It has **a tear** in it./There's **a hole** in it.
The car is **damaged**.	There is **some damage** on the bumper.
The coffee mug is **chipped**.	There is **a chip** in it.
My pants are **stained**.	They have **a stain** on them.
The camera lens is **scratched**.	There are **a few scratches** on it.
The washing machine **is leaking**.*	It has **a leak**.

**Exception:* is leaking *is a present continuous form.*

GRAMMAR PLUS *see page 137*

A Read the comments from customers in a restaurant. Write sentences in two different ways using forms of the word in parentheses. Then compare with a partner.

1. Could we have another water pitcher? This one . . . (crack)
2. That valet was so careless. My car . . . (dent)
3. The toilet is dirty. And the sink . . . (leak)
4. This tablecloth isn't very clean. It . . . (stain)
5. Would you bring me another glass? This glass . . . (chip)
6. The table looks pretty dirty. The wood . . . , too. (scratch)
7. The server needs a new shirt. The one he's wearing . . . (tear)
8. The walls really need paint. And the ceiling . . . (damage)

1. *This one is cracked.*
   It has a crack.

B **PAIR WORK** Describe two problems with each thing below. Use forms of the words in the box. You may use the same word more than once.

break	crack	damage	dent	leak	scratch	stain	tear

1
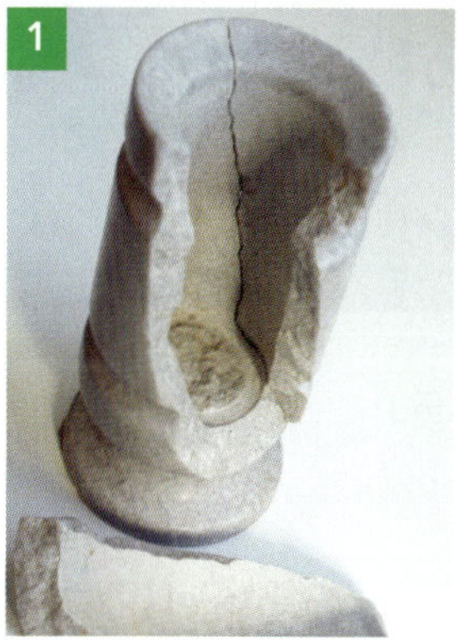
2

3

4
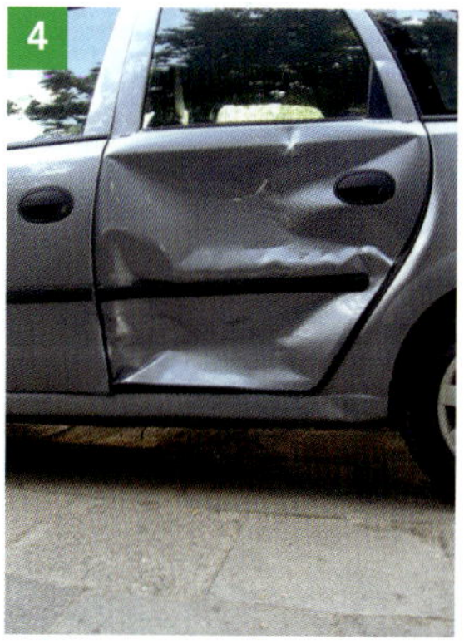

A: The vase is broken.
B: Yes. And it has a crack, too.

C **GROUP WORK** Look around your classroom. How many problems can you describe?

"The floor is scratched, and the window is cracked. The desks are . . ."

4 LISTENING I'd like a refund.

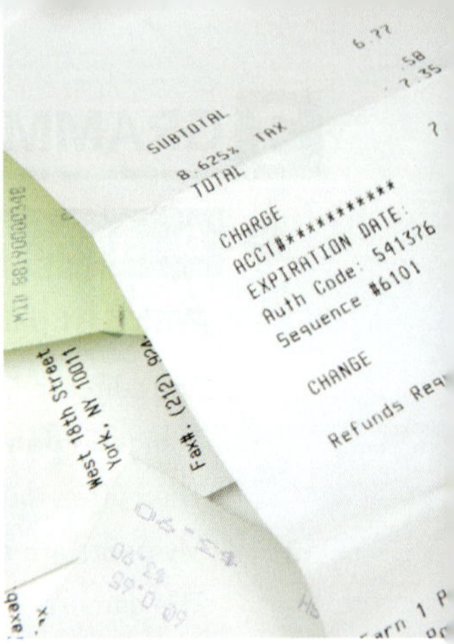

A Listen to three customers return items they purchased. Complete the chart.

	Did the store give a refund?	Why or why not?
1. Evie		
2. Darren		
3. Gisela		

B **GROUP WORK** How is your culture similar or different in terms of refunds and customer service?

5 ROLE PLAY How can I help you?

Student A: You are returning an item to a store. Decide what the item is and explain why you are returning it.

Student B: You are a salesperson. A customer is returning an item to the store. Ask these questions:

What exactly is the problem?
Can you show it to me?
Was it like this when you bought it?
When did you buy it?
Do you have the receipt?
Would you like a refund or a store credit?

Change roles and try the role play again.

6 CONVERSATION It needs to be adjusted.

A Listen and practice.

MR. LEROY Hello?

HEATHER Hello, Mr. Leroy. This is Heather Forman.

MR. LEROY Uh, Ms. Forman . . .

HEATHER In Apartment 12C.

MR. LEROY Oh, yes. What can I do for you? Does your refrigerator need fixing again?

HEATHER No, it's the oven this time.

MR. LEROY Oh. So, what's wrong with it?

HEATHER Well, I think the temperature control needs to be adjusted. The oven keeps burning everything I try to cook.

MR. LEROY Really? OK, I'll have someone look at it right away.

HEATHER Thanks a lot, Mr. Leroy.

MR. LEROY Uh, by the way, Ms. Forman, are you sure it's the oven and not your cooking?

B Listen to another tenant's call with Mr. Leroy. What's the tenant's problem?

7 GRAMMAR FOCUS

Describing problems 2

Need + gerund	*Need* + passive infinitive	*Keep* + gerund
The oven **needs adjusting**.	It **needs to be adjusted**.	Everything **keeps burning**.
The alarm **needs fixing**.	It **needs to be fixed**.	The alarm **keeps going off**.

GRAMMAR PLUS *see page 137*

A What needs to be done in this apartment? Write sentences about these items using *need* with gerunds or passive infinitives.

1. the cupboards (clean)
2. the fire alarm (adjust)
3. the lights (replace)
4. the plants (water)
5. the oven (fix)
6. the ceiling (paint)
7. the window (wash)
8. the light switch (change)

1. The cupboards need cleaning.
OR
1. The cupboards need to be cleaned.

B **PAIR WORK** Think of five improvements you would like to make in your home. Which improvements will you most likely make? Which won't you make?

"First, the bedroom walls need painting. There are some small cracks. . . ."

8 WORD POWER Problems with electronics

A Circle the correct gerund to complete the sentences. Then compare with a partner.

1. My TV screen goes on and off all the time. It keeps **flickering** / **sticking**.
2. The music player app jumps to the next song every 20 seconds. It keeps **crashing** / **skipping**.
3. The battery in my new camera doesn't last long. It keeps **freezing** / **dying**.
4. Something is wrong with my computer! It keeps **crashing** / **jamming**.
5. I can't talk for long on my new phone. It keeps **dying** / **dropping** calls.
6. This printer isn't making all the copies I want. It keeps **jamming** / **flickering**.
7. My computer needs to be replaced. It keeps **dropping** / **freezing**.
8. The buttons on the remote control don't work well. They keep **skipping** / **sticking**.

B **GROUP WORK** Describe a problem with an electronic item you own. Don't identify it! Others will try to guess the item.

"Some keys on my device keep sticking, and some are loose. . . ."

9 PRONUNCIATION Contrastive stress

A Listen and practice. Notice how a change in stress changes the meaning of each question and elicits a different response.

Is the **bed**room window cracked? (No, the kitchen window is cracked.)

Is the bedroom **win**dow cracked? (No, the bedroom door is cracked.)

Is the bedroom window **cracked**? (No, it's stuck.)

B Listen to the questions. Check (✓) the correct response.

1. a. Are my jeans torn?
- ☐ No, they're stained.
- ☐ No, your shirt is torn.

b. Are my jeans torn?
- ☐ No, they're stained.
- ☐ No, your shirt is torn.

2. a. Is the computer screen flickering?
- ☐ No, it's freezing.
- ☐ No, the TV screen is flickering.

b. Is the computer screen flickering?
- ☐ No, it's freezing.
- ☐ No, the TV screen is flickering.

10 LISTENING A throwaway culture

A Listen to a conversation between two friends. Answer the questions.

1. What is wrong with Hayley's phone? ____________
2. What is Hayley's solution? ____________
3. What is Aaron's solution? ____________
4. Why doesn't Hayley like Aaron's solution? ____________

B Listen again. What is a "throwaway culture"?

C **GROUP WORK** Do you agree that electronics aren't made as well as they used to be? Give an example to support your opinion.

11 WRITING A critical online review

A Imagine that you ordered a product online, but when you received it, you were unhappy with it. Write a critical online review. Explain all of the problems with the product and why you think others shouldn't buy it.

> **Best 4U promises a lot, delivers nothing.**
>
> I ordered a phone from Best 4U's website for my son's birthday. First, it took six weeks for the company to send it, and it arrived two weeks after his birthday. Now, the battery keeps dying very fast when he's just watching a movie or . . . READ MORE

B **GROUP WORK** Read your classmates' reviews. What would you do if you read this critical online review and worked for the company that sold the product?

12 INTERCHANGE 6 Home makeover

Do you have an eye for detail? Student A, go to Interchange 6A on page 119; Student B, go to Interchange 6B on page 120.

13 READING

A Skim the advice column. What problem did the reader have? How does the writer suggest solving the problem?

Home | Local | World | Entertainment | Advice column

Ask the Fixer!

Our problem-solver Marci Davis addresses a common problem with ride-sharing services.

After a meeting downtown, I used my phone to book a ride with a private car service in order to get home. As soon as the pick-up was confirmed, a friend came out of the building, spotted me, and offered me a ride home. I immediately canceled the car. But the next day I got an alert on my phone – the car service had charged my credit card $10! I contacted the service, and they said it was for a late cancellation. I didn't realize they were going to charge me for that! Can you fix this? – Lawrence, New York City

The fact is, Lawrence, that you need to read the terms of your ride-sharing app. It states clearly – somewhere in all those thousands of words – that when you cancel your ride less than ten minutes before your car is scheduled to arrive, you have to pay a fee. After all, the driver has already refused other possible passengers and is driving in your direction, so it's a loss when you cancel.

On the other hand, I do think something needs to be fixed. Do you know anyone who reads all the way through the terms of use for any app? There isn't enough time in the day! I talked to a representative at your ride-sharing company and made two suggestions. First, they need to highlight their cancellation policy at the beginning of the terms, where people will see it. Then, when you cancel a ride, a notification needs to be sent that tells you about the cancellation charge. That way, riders won't keep getting this annoying surprise. Let's hope the company pays attention.

What do you think? Post your comments, suggestions, complaints, and anecdotes.

B Read the advice column. Find the words in italics in the article. Then check (✓) the meaning of each word.

1. *confirm*	☐ make something available	☐ state that something will happen
2. *cancellation*	☐ act of stopping something	☐ act of delaying something
3. *representative*	☐ person who speaks for a company	☐ person who owns a company
4. *terms*	☐ rules of an agreement	☐ features of an app
5. *notification*	☐ act of giving information	☐ act of asking a question

C For each statement, check (✓) True, False, or Not given.

	True	False	Not given
1. Lawrence booked a ride by mistake.	☐	☐	☐
2. Lawrence did not expect to be charged for his ride.	☐	☐	☐
3. The cancellation rule is available to read on the app.	☐	☐	☐
4. Marci Davis thinks the cancellation fee is too expensive.	☐	☐	☐
5. The company representative apologized for what happened.	☐	☐	☐
6. Marci says ride-sharing agreements should be more clear.	☐	☐	☐

D Have you ever used a ride-sharing service? What do you think of this type of service?

Units 5–6 Progress check

SELF-ASSESSMENT

How well can you do these things? Check (✓) the boxes.

I can . . .	Very well	OK	A little
Talk about feelings and expectations (Ex. 1)	☐	☐	☐
Discuss cultural differences (Ex. 2)	☐	☐	☐
Understand problems and complaints (Ex. 3)	☐	☐	☐
Describe problems (Ex. 4)	☐	☐	☐
Discuss what needs to be improved (Ex. 5)	☐	☐	☐

1 SPEAKING Facing new challenges

PAIR WORK Choose a situation. Then ask your partner questions about it using the words in the box. Take turns.

moving to another city
going to a new school
starting a new job
getting married

anxious	**excited**
curious	**insecure**
embarrassed	**nervous**
enthusiastic	**worried**

A: If you were moving to another city, what would you be nervous about?

B: One thing I'd be nervous about is not having any friends around. I'd be worried about feeling lonely!

2 SURVEY Cultural behavior

A What do you think of these behaviors? Complete the survey.

Is it acceptable to . . . ?	Yes	No	It depends
give money as a gift	☐	☐	☐
call older people by their first names	☐	☐	☐
greet friends with a kiss on the cheek	☐	☐	☐
ask how old someone is	☐	☐	☐
put your feet on the furniture	☐	☐	☐

B **GROUP WORK** Compare your opinions. When are these behaviors acceptable? When are they unacceptable? What behaviors are never acceptable?

A: It's not acceptable to give money as a gift.

B: Oh, I think it depends. I think it's OK to give money to kids and teens, and as a wedding gift, but . . .

3 LISTENING I have a problem.

A Listen to three tenants complain to their building manager. Complete the chart.

	Tenant's complaint	How the problem is solved
1.		
2.		
3.		

B GROUP WORK Do you agree with the solutions? How would you solve the problems?

4 ROLE PLAY Haggling

Student A: You want to buy this car from Student B, but it's too expensive. Describe the problems you see to get a better price.

Student B: You are trying to sell this car, but it has some problems. Make excuses for the problems to get the most money.

A: I'm interested in this car, but the door handle is broken. I'll give you $ . . . for it.

B: That's no big deal. You can fix that easily. How about $ . . . ?

A: Well, what about the windshield? It's . . .

B: You can't really see that. . . .

Change roles and try the role play again.

5 DISCUSSION School improvements

A GROUP WORK Imagine you are on a school improvement committee. You are discussing changes to your school. Decide on the five biggest issues.

A: The Wi-Fi connection needs to be improved. It keeps disconnecting, and it's not fast enough.

B: Yes, but it's more important to replace the couch in the student lounge. It has a big hole and stains.

B CLASS ACTIVITY Share your list with the class. What are the three most needed improvements? Can you think of how to accomplish them?

WHAT'S NEXT?

Look at your Self-assessment again. Do you need to review anything?

7 What can we do?

- Discuss environmental problems
- Compare solutions to social problems

1 SNAPSHOT

WHAT A WASTE!

The United States generates **254 million** tons of waste a year.
The average American produces almost **2** kilograms of waste a day.

Fifteen hundred plastic bottles are consumed every second in the United States.
It takes at least **500** years for a plastic bottle to decompose.

Americans throw away around **130 million** cell phones a year.
Much of this e-waste ends up in landfills.

In the U.S., **30–40%** of the food supply is wasted.
That could feed **millions** of hungry people.

How could we reduce the waste of each of these items?
What do you throw away? What do you tend to recycle?
What are two other environmental problems that concern you?

2 PERSPECTIVES Vote for a better city!

A Listen to an announcement from an election campaign. What kinds of problems does Grace Medina want to fix?

VOTE FOR GRACE MEDINA FOR CITY COUNCIL

Grace Medina's ideas for Riverside!

Have you noticed these problems in our city?

- Our fresh water supply is being contaminated by toxic chemicals.
- The roads aren't being repaired due to a lack of funding.
- Our community center has been closed because of high maintenance costs.
- Our city streets are being damaged as a result of heavy traffic.
- Many public parks have been lost through overbuilding.
- Low-income families are being displaced from their homes due to high rental prices.

GRACE MEDINA – THE CHANGE WE NEED

B Which of these problems affect your city? Can you give specific examples?

3 GRAMMAR FOCUS

Passive with prepositions

Present continuous passive

Our water supply **is being contaminated** **by** toxic chemicals.
Our city streets **are being damaged** **as a result of** heavy traffic.
The roads **aren't being repaired** **due to** a lack of funding.

Present perfect passive

Our community center **has been closed** **because of** high costs.
Many public parks **have been lost** **through** overbuilding.

GRAMMAR PLUS *see page 138*

A PAIR WORK Match the photos of environmental problems with the sentences below.

1. High emissions of carbon dioxide are causing climate changes. (by)
2. Rapid urbanization is depleting our natural resources. (through)
3. Water pollution has threatened the health of people all over the world. (due to)
4. Livestock farms have contaminated the soil and underground water. (because of)
5. The destruction of rain forests is accelerating the extinction of plants and wildlife. (as a result of)
6. Oil spills are harming birds, fish, and other marine life. (through)

B Rewrite the sentences in part A using the passive and the prepositions given. Then compare with a partner.

1. *Climate changes are being caused by high emissions of carbon dioxide.*

C PAIR WORK Cover the sentences in part A above. Take turns describing the environmental problems in the pictures in your own words.

4 PRONUNCIATION Reduction of auxiliary verbs

A Listen and practice. Notice how the auxiliary verb forms **is**, **are**, **has**, and **have** are reduced in conversation.

Food **is** being wasted.	Our community center **has** been closed.
Streets **are** being damaged.	Parks **have** been lost.

B **PAIR WORK** Practice the sentences you wrote in Exercise 3, part B. Pay attention to the reduction of **is**, **are**, **has**, and **have**.

5 LISTENING Saving the environment

A Listen to three people describe some serious environmental problems. Check (✓) the problem each person talks about.

	Problem		What can be done about it?
1. Morgan	☐ landfills	☐ poor farmland	
2. Dalton	☐ electricity	☐ e-waste	
3. Kendall	☐ air pollution	☐ water pollution	

B Listen again. What can be done to solve each problem? Complete the chart.

C **GROUP WORK** Which problem above worries you the most? What is being done to fix it?

6 WORD POWER Global challenges

A **PAIR WORK** How concerned is your partner about these problems? Check (✓) his or her answers.

Problems	Very concerned	Fairly concerned	Not concerned
unemployment	☐	☐	☐
famine	☐	☐	☐
global warming	☐	☐	☐
government corruption	☐	☐	☐
infectious diseases	☐	☐	☐
political unrest	☐	☐	☐
poverty	☐	☐	☐
recession	☐	☐	☐
violence	☐	☐	☐

B **GROUP WORK** Share your partner's answers with another pair. Which problems concern your group the most? What will happen if the problem isn't solved?

A: Many people have been affected by the high rates of unemployment.
B: We need to create more jobs and invest in education.
C: I agree. If we don't, young people won't have any opportunities in the future.

7 CONVERSATION What if it doesn't work?

A Listen and practice.

Cindy: Did you hear about the dead fish that were found floating in the Bush River this morning?
Otis: Yeah, I read something about it. Do you know what happened?
Cindy: Well, there's a factory outside town that's pumping chemicals into the river.
Otis: How can they do that? Isn't that against the law?
Cindy: Yes, it is. But a lot of companies ignore those laws.
Otis: That's terrible! What can we do about it?
Cindy: Well, one way to change things is to talk to the company's management.
Otis: What if that doesn't work?
Cindy: Well, then another way to stop them is to get a news station to run a story on it.
Otis: Yes! Companies hate bad publicity. By the way, what's the name of this company?
Cindy: Believe it or not, it's called Green Mission Industries.
Otis: Really? My uncle is one of their top executives.

B **CLASS ACTIVITY** What else could Cindy and Otis do?

C Listen to the rest of the conversation. What do Cindy and Otis decide to do?

8 GRAMMAR FOCUS

Infinitive clauses and phrases

One way **to change** things is	**to talk** to the company's management.
Another way **to stop** them is	**to get** a news station to run a story.
The best ways **to fight** unemployment are	**to create** more jobs and invest in education.

GRAMMAR PLUS *see page 138*

A Find one or more solutions for each problem. Then compare with a partner.

Problems

1. The best way to fight poverty is ______
2. One way to reduce government corruption is ______
3. One way to reduce unemployment is ______
4. The best way to stop global warming is ______
5. One way to help the homeless is ______
6. One way to improve air quality is ______

Solutions

a. to provide more affordable housing.
b. to create more jobs.
c. to make politicians accountable for decisions.
d. to have more vocational training programs.
e. to increase the use of cleaner energy.
f. to provide education to all children.
g. to build more public shelters.
h. to reduce deforestation.

B **GROUP WORK** Can you think of two more solutions for each problem in part A? Agree on the best solution for each.

9 DISCUSSION What should be done?

A **GROUP WORK** Describe the problems shown in the photos. Then make suggestions about how to solve these problems.

What can be done . . . ?

1. to reduce crime
2. to keep our water supplies safe
3. to improve children's health
4. to improve traffic and mobility

A: Our cities are being taken over by criminals.
B: Well, one way to fight crime is to have more police on the streets.
C: That's not enough. The best way to stop it is . . .

B **CLASS ACTIVITY** Share your solutions. Which ones are the most innovative? Which ones are most likely to solve the problems?

10 INTERCHANGE 7 Take action!

Brainstorm solutions to some local problems. Go to Interchange 7 on page 121.

11 WRITING A post on a community website

A Choose one of the problems from the unit or use one of your own ideas. Write a message to post on a community website.

NO MORE **JUNK FOOD!**

Our schools are serving poor quality food to our children. School cafeterias offer mostly fast food and soda to students. This has to change. One way to change this is . . .

B **PAIR WORK** Exchange messages with a partner. Write a response suggesting another solution to his or her problem.

12 READING

A Skim the article. What problem did the island face? What solution did the inhabitants come up with?

Home | News | Feature stories | Sign in | Community

TURNING AN INVASION INTO AN ADVANTAGE

Lionfish are beautiful creatures. They are also one of the most invasive and destructive sea creatures on the planet, causing particularly serious problems in the Caribbean Sea. Their numbers have increased dramatically in a few years there, and they have already caused a great deal of damage to the ecosystem.

St. Lucia is a Caribbean island where action is being taken against the invasive species. The island is famous for its clear blue waters, and many tourists enjoy diving in order to explore the wonders of the extensive coral reefs. Unfortunately, lionfish eat the native fish that keep the reefs clean and healthy, putting the reefs at risk. It is estimated that lionfish can eat up to 80% of the small fish in a coral reef in five weeks, and because the invasive fish reproduce very quickly the problem could easily get worse in no time.

Instead of trying to trap or poison the destructive fish, islanders are turning the lionfish invasion to their advantage. They realized that one way to reduce the population of lionfish was to hunt them for sport and business, and then use them for food. Although the fish have a very poisonous sting, they can be prepared so they are safe to eat. And Caribbean cooks were sure to find a way to turn these unwelcome fish into an unforgettable treat.

Unfortunately, the lionfish population has not been reduced by much, but at least the fish have been kept from multiplying too quickly. Jobs have also been provided for unemployed fishermen, who were unable to fish for other types of sea life in the protected waters. The lionfish are still a problem, but the islanders are making the best of a bad situation – and they are making a living from it, too!

B Read the article. Answer the questions.

1. Why are the lionfish a concern?
2. Why is it important to protect the area around St. Lucia?
3. What characteristic makes the lionfish hard to control?
4. What solutions have the islanders come up with?
5. What have the results of the islanders' efforts been?

C **GROUP WORK** What environmental threats exist where you live? Can you think of any creative or unusual ways to deal with them?

8 Never stop learning.

- Discuss personal preferences
- Discuss ways of learning and life skills

1 SNAPSHOT

Learning: Anywhere, Anytime, for Any Reason

LEARNING PATHS

go to college
take online courses
take traditional training classes
study on your own
set up a study group
attend conferences
watch filmed lectures

LEARNING BENEFITS

get a degree
meet people and expand your network
change jobs or career path
get a raise or promotion at work
get a professional license or certification
learn something that makes your life easier
have fun

Which learning paths have you tried? How was your experience?
Which learning benefits do you consider the most important? Why?
Are you planning to learn anything new this year? What?

2 PERSPECTIVES A survey

A Listen to a survey that a school is conducting about student preferences. Check (✓) the student's answers.

Springfield Center for Continuing Education

New courses survey

1. Would you rather study on your own or join a study group?
- ☐ **a.** I'd rather study on my own.
- ☐ **b.** I'd rather join a study group.
- ☐ **c.** I'd rather do both.

2. Would you rather take an art course or a professional course?
- ☐ **a.** I'd rather take an art course.
- ☐ **b.** I'd rather take a professional course.
- ☐ **c.** I'd rather not take either. I'd rather <u>take a language course</u>.

3. Would you prefer to take an online course or a traditional course?
- ☐ **a.** I'd prefer to take an online course.
- ☐ **b.** I'd prefer to take a traditional course.
- ☐ **c.** I'd prefer not to take either. I'd prefer to <u>hire a private tutor</u>.

B **PAIR WORK** Take the survey. You can change the underlined information. Discuss your answers with a partner.

3 PRONUNCIATION Intonation in questions of choice

Listen and practice. Notice the intonation in questions of choice.

Would you prefer to study online or at a school?

Would you rather learn something fun or useful?

4 GRAMMAR FOCUS

Would rather and *would prefer*

Would rather **takes the base form of the verb.** ***Would prefer*** **usually takes an infinitive. Both are followed by** ***not*** **in the negative.**

Would you **rather take** an art course or a professional course?

I'd rather take an art course.

I'd rather not take either.

I'd rather take a language course than study art.

Let's join a study group.

I'd rather not join a group.

I'd rather not.

I'd prefer not to join a group.

I'd prefer not to.

Would you prefer to take an online course or a traditional course?

I'd prefer to take an online course. **I'd prefer not to take** either.

GRAMMAR PLUS *see page 139*

A Complete the conversations with *would* and the appropriate forms of the verbs in parentheses. Then practice with a partner.

1. **A:** ______________ you rather ______________ (take) a technical course or an art course?
   B: I would prefer ______________ (take) an art course. I'd like to learn to paint.
2. **A:** ______________ you prefer ______________ (get) a promotion or a new job?
   B: Actually, I'm not very happy at my present job, so I'd rather ______________ (get) a new job.
3. **A:** ______________ you prefer ______________ (learn) something fun or something practical?
   B: I guess I'd prefer ______________ (study) something practical, like personal finance.
4. **A:** ______________ you rather ______________ (learn) English in England or Canada?
   B: To tell you the truth, I'd prefer ______________ (not study) in either place. I'd rather ______________ (go) to Australia because it's warmer there.
5. **A:** If you decided to learn to play an instrument, ______________ you prefer ______________ (attend) a class or ______________ (have) a private tutor?
   B: I'd rather ______________ (take) a class than ______________ (hire) a tutor.
6. **A:** ______________ you rather ______________ (have) a job in an office or ______________ (work) outdoors?
   B: I'd definitely rather ______________ (have) a job where I'm outdoors.

B **PAIR WORK** Take turns asking the questions in part A. Pay attention to intonation. Give your own information when responding.

5 LISTENING Do what you love.

A Listen to a conversation between a student and his guidance counselor. Check (✓) the suggestions the guidance counselor gives.

- [ ] talking to professors
- [ ] job shadowing
- [ ] volunteer work
- [ ] informational interviews
- [ ] more classes
- [ ] internships

B **PAIR WORK** If you could learn more about a job, what job would it be? Why? Which options above would you use?

6 SPEAKING Learn something new

A **GROUP WORK** Think of a personal or professional skill you would like to learn or improve. Discuss how you are planning to learn it. Use the ideas from the Snapshot on page 50, or use your own ideas.

A: I want to speak Italian. I think I'm going to take an online course.
B: It's hard to learn a language online. I think you should go to a language school.
A: I don't know. I'm really shy. I'd rather not have classes with other people.
C: You could . . .

B **CLASS ACTIVITY** Share your ideas with your classmates. Who is going to learn something unusual? How are they going to learn it?

7 INTERCHANGE 8 Making choices

What would you most like to learn? Take a survey. Go to Interchange 8 on page 122.

8 CONVERSATION It works for me.

A Listen and practice.

Marta: So how's your Mandarin class going?
Kevin: Harder than I expected, actually. I'm finding the pronunciation very difficult.
Marta: Well, I imagine it takes a while to get it right. You know, you could improve your accent by watching movies.
Kevin: That's a good idea. But how do you learn new vocabulary? I always seem to forget new words.
Marta: I learn new English words best by writing them down and reviewing them many times. I've been using this vocabulary-building app. It really works for me. Look.
Kevin: Hmm. Maybe I should try something like that!

B Listen to two other students, Rick and Nia, explain how they learn new words. Who uses technology to study? Who organizes words by category?

C **CLASS ACTIVITY** How do you learn new words in a foreign language?

9 GRAMMAR FOCUS

By + gerund to describe how to do things

You could improve your accent **by watching** movies.
I learn new words best **by writing** them down and **reviewing** them many times.
The best way to learn slang is not **by watching** the news but **by watching** TV series.

GRAMMAR PLUS see page 139

A How can you improve your English? Complete the sentences with *by* and the gerund forms of the verbs. Then compare with a partner.

1. A good way to learn idioms is ________________ (watch) American sitcoms.
2. The best way to practice what you have learned is ________________ (use) it in messages or conversation.
3. Students can become better writers ________________ (read) more.
4. You can learn to use grammar correctly ________________ (do) grammar exercises online.
5. The best way to develop self-confidence in communication is ________________ (talk) with native speakers.
6. You can improve your accent ________________ (listen) to songs and singing along.
7. A good way to memorize new vocabulary is ________________ (play) vocabulary games.
8. You could become a more fluent reader ________________ (read) something you're interested in every day.

B **GROUP WORK** Complete the sentences in part A with your own ideas. What's the best suggestion for each item?

A: In my opinion, a good way to learn idioms is by talking to native speakers.
B: I think the best way is not by talking to native speakers but by watching TV shows.

10 DISCUSSION Learning styles

A Listen to James and Sophia describe how they developed two skills. How did they learn? Complete the chart.

	James	Sophia
1. become an effective public speaker		
2. learn to drive		

B **GROUP WORK** How would *you* learn to do the things in the chart?

C **GROUP WORK** Talk about different ways to learn to do each of these activities. Then agree on the most effective method.

take professional-looking photos
manage your time
cook
become a good conversationalist
break dance
swim
play a musical instrument

11 WORD POWER Life skills

A **PAIR WORK** How do we learn each of these things? Check (✓) your opinions.

	From parents	From school	On our own
communication skills	☐	☐	☐
competitiveness	☐	☐	☐
concern for others	☐	☐	☐
cooperation	☐	☐	☐
creativity	☐	☐	☐
money management	☐	☐	☐
perseverance	☐	☐	☐
problem solving	☐	☐	☐
self-confidence	☐	☐	☐
self-discipline	☐	☐	☐
time management	☐	☐	☐
tolerance	☐	☐	☐

some activities

using a daily planner
volunteering in a hospital
taking a public speaking class
performing in a play
going to museums
learning a martial art
playing a team sport
making a budget

B **GROUP WORK** How can you develop the skills in part A? Use the activities in the box or your own ideas.

A: You can develop communication skills by taking a public speaking class.

B: You can also develop them by trying to be a better listener.

12 WRITING Something I learned

A Think of a skill you have learned. Read these questions and take notes. Then use your notes to write about what you learned.

What is required to be successful at it?
What are some ways people learn to do it?
How did you learn it?
What was difficult about learning it?

I used to have serious problems managing my finances, and I never paid my bills on time. I have to admit I had very poor money management skills. Some people learn to manage their money at home or by taking courses at school, but I didn't.

When a friend told me about a personal finance course, I decided to take it. I first learned to keep track of my expenses by recording every penny I spent. Then . . .

B **GROUP WORK** Share your writing. Have any of your classmates' experiences inspired you to learn a new skill?

13 READING

A Have you ever had trouble focusing when you're studying? What did you do about it?

Are you studying the "right" way?

Home | News | Articles | Sign in | Community   Search

You may study differently from your friends, but your study habits are probably not wrong!

Kelly and Maria are best friends with a lot in common. They love doing things together, such as going to movies and concerts, shopping, or just sitting at a local café. Since they take a lot of the same school subjects, they would love to study together, but they find this impossible. Their working styles are so completely different that they can't be in the same room while they are studying!

Kelly would rather study in a clean, open space, whereas Maria works best by surrounding herself with books, papers, and other clutter. Kelly prefers to study in a totally silent room, but Maria loves to play music or even have the TV on. Kelly can sit for hours without moving, and often gets all of her homework done in one sitting. Maria, on the other hand, is constantly getting up, and claims that she thinks best when she's on the move.

You might be asking yourself, which way of studying gets better results? Many people assume that a silent, uncluttered setting is the way to go, but it seems that is not necessarily the case. Some research has even shown that outside noise and clutter help some people concentrate because it makes them form a mental "wall" around what they are doing and improves their focus. So, if you're a student who chooses to study while sitting at a table in a busy shopping mall, don't worry about it. And if you work in total silence, that's OK, too. Judging from Kelly and Maria's study habits, the best way to study is the way that works for you. With their very different approaches, both of them do extremely well in school, and both finish their work in about the same amount of time as well.

One curious fact about the two friends: Despite their opposing studying styles, they have almost identical ambitions. Both are planning to go to law school – Kelly with the idea of becoming a human rights attorney and Maria hoping to become a public defender. But will they be study buddies? Not a chance!

B Read the article. Find the words in *italics* in the article. Then match each word with its meaning.

1. *clutter* ______
2. *sitting* ______
3. *concentrate* ______
4. *approach* ______
5. *identical* ______

a. focus attention on something
b. exactly the same
c. period of activity without a break
d. way of doing something
e. objects in a state of disorder

C Complete the summary with information from the article. Use one or two words in each blank.

Kelly and Maria are friends who have a lot ______________, but they can't study together because they have ______________. Kelly likes a ______________ that is very quiet, and she can ______________ for a long time. Maria prefers a space that is ______________, and she likes to ______________. Studies show that neither way of studying is ______________ than the other. Noise can help some people ______________, for example. Despite their different habits, Kelly and Maria are both ______________ students, and it is interesting that the friends have ______________ plans for the future.

D **GROUP WORK** Whose studying style is closest to yours, Kelly's or Maria's? Why?

Units 7–8 Progress check

SELF-ASSESSMENT

How well can you do these things? Check (✓) the boxes.

I can . . .	Very well	OK	A little
Describe environmental problems (Ex. 1)	☐	☐	☐
Discuss solutions to problems (Ex. 2)	☐	☐	☐
Understand examples of personal qualities (Ex. 3)	☐	☐	☐
Discuss personal preferences (Ex. 4)	☐	☐	☐

1 SPEAKING Environmental issues

PAIR WORK Choose a probable cause for each of the problems and discuss possible solutions.

PROBLEM

- Forests are being destroyed.
- The quality of the air is being lowered.
- Marine life is being affected.
- Water is being contaminated.
- Landfills are overflowing.
- City streets are being damaged.

CAUSE

- the lack of recycling
- heavy traffic
- rapid urbanization
- climate changes
- fumes from cars
- factory waste

A: Forests are being destroyed because of rapid urbanization.
B: We need plans for urban development that don't . . .

2 DISCUSSION Tricky social situations

A PAIR WORK Read these problems that friends sometimes have with each other. Suggest solutions for each problem.

Your friend is always criticizing you and your other friends.
Your best friend never pays for his or her share at group dinners.
A friend is having a party and you weren't invited.

B GROUP WORK Agree on the best solution for each problem.

"The best thing to do is to talk to your friend and say how you feel."

useful expressions

One thing to do is to . . .
Another way to help is to . . .
The best thing to do is . . .

3 LISTENING I got it!

A Listen to people talk about recent events and activities in their lives. What events and activities are they talking about? What two qualities does each person's behavior demonstrate? Complete the chart.

a. money management
b. competitiveness
c. creativity
d. concern for others
e. perseverance
f. self-confidence

	Event or activity	Qualities
1. Kate		*e,*
2. Mark		
3. Iris		

B **PAIR WORK** Describe a time when you demonstrated one of the qualities above. Can your partner guess the quality?

4 QUESTIONNAIRE Learning styles

A **PAIR WORK** Interview your partner. Circle the ways your partner prefers to improve his or her English.

1. When you don't understand a word, would you prefer to . . . ?
a. look it up in a dictionary or **b.** try to guess the meaning

2. If you don't understand what someone says, would you rather . . . ?
a. ask the person to repeat it or **b.** pretend you understand

3. When you hear a new word in English, would you rather . . . ?
a. write it down or **b.** try to remember it

4. When you make a mistake in English, would you prefer someone to . . . ?
a. correct it immediately or **b.** ignore it

5. When you meet a native English speaker, would you prefer to . . . ?
a. try to talk to the person or **b.** listen while he or she speaks

6. When you have to contact someone in English, would you rather . . . ?
a. call him or her on the phone or **b.** send him or her an email

"I'd prefer to try to guess the meaning of a new word."

B **GROUP WORK** Discuss the advantages and disadvantages of each option in part A. Are there better options for each situation?

A: When I try to guess the meaning of a new word, it takes less time, so I can read faster.
B: Yes, but if you look it up, you learn a new word.
C: I think the best way to deal with a new word is to try and guess the meaning, and then check if it makes sense.

WHAT'S NEXT?

Look at your Self-assessment again. Do you need to review anything?

9 Getting things done

- Discuss professional services
- Make suggestions

1 SNAPSHOT

Why would someone need these services? Have you ever used any of them?
How do you choose a company or person to do any of these services?

2 PERSPECTIVES Get the job done!

A Listen to an advertisement. Would you use a service like this? Why or why not?

Leave It to Me!

Let us handle your to-do list. Tell us what you need done, and we'll find the right people to do the job for you.

Home services

Get your apartment cleaned and your belongings organized.
Have your walls painted and your leaking sink fixed.
Get all your home appliances repaired.

Everyday errands and odd jobs

Want to have your car washed and waxed? Need help preparing a meal for your family? Don't have time to wait in line? Too busy to pick up cat food or drop off your laundry? You can have it all done at affordable prices.

Download the Leave It to Me app and get 10% off your first hour of work.

B What services do you need or want? What questions would you ask before hiring a person to do these services for you?

3 GRAMMAR FOCUS

Get or have something done

Use *get* or *have*, the object, and the past participle of the verb to describe a service performed for you by someone else.

Do something yourself	*Get/have something done for you*
I **clean** my house every week.	I **get** my house **cleaned** (by a cleaner) every week.
He **is painting** his bedroom.	He **is having** his bedroom **painted**.
They **fixed** the sink.	They **got** the sink **fixed**.
Did you **paint** your bedroom?	Did you **have** your bedroom **painted**?
Where can I **wash** my car?	Where can I **have** my car **washed**?

GRAMMAR PLUS *see page 140*

A Complete the sentences to express that the services are performed by someone else.

1. My parents didn't paint their house before they moved in. They ___had it painted___. (have)
2. I didn't repair my own laptop. I ______________ at the electronics store. (get)
3. Many people don't wash their cars. They ______________. (have)
4. My bedroom carpet is very dirty, but I'm not cleaning it. I'm ______________ next week. (get)
5. My brother isn't repairing his bike. He ______________. (have)

B **PAIR WORK** Take turns describing the services in the pictures.

1. Jessica

2. Peter

3. Zoey

4. Tricia

"Jessica is having her nails done."

C **PAIR WORK** Tell your partner about three things you've had done for you recently. Ask and answer questions for more information.

4 PRONUNCIATION Sentence stress

A Listen and practice. Notice that when the object becomes a pronoun (sentence B), it is no longer stressed.

A: Where can I have my car washed?
B: You can have it washed at the auto shop.

A: Where can I get my nails done?
B: You can get them done at a salon.

B **GROUP WORK** Ask questions about three things you want to have done. Pay attention to sentence stress. Other students give answers.

5 DISCUSSION On demand

PAIR WORK Are these services available in your city? For those that aren't, do you think they would be a good idea?

Can you . . . ?

get groceries delivered to your door
have a five-star meal cooked at your home by a chef
have your home organized by a professional organizer
have your portrait drawn by a street artist
get your pet vaccinated at home
get your blood pressure checked at a pharmacy
have your shoes shined on the street
get your car washed for less than $15
have a suit made in under 24 hours
have pizza delivered after midnight

A: Can you get groceries delivered to your door?
B: Sure! You can have it done by . . .

6 INTERCHANGE 9 Absolutely not!

What do parents and teenagers usually argue about? Go to Interchange 9 on page 123.

7 WORD POWER Three-word phrasal verbs

A Match each phrasal verb in these sentences with its meaning. Then compare with a partner.

Phrasal verbs

1. Polly has **broken up with** her boyfriend. ______
2. Lin **came up with** a great idea for a new app for meeting people. ______
3. My brother is **looking forward to** getting married. He really loves his fiancée. ______
4. I can't **keep up with** all the new technology. It changes so fast. ______
5. Luisa doesn't **get along with** her roommate. They argue over every little thing. ______
6. My doctor says I'm overweight. I should **cut down on** sweets. ______
7. I can't **put up with** the noise on my street! I'll have to move. ______
8. I don't like to **take care of** my own finances. I have an accountant manage my money. ______

Meanings

a. reduce the quantity of
b. end a romantic relationship with
c. continue to learn about
d. tolerate
e. be excited for
f. have a good relationship with
g. be responsible for
h. think of; develop

B **PAIR WORK** Take turns making sentences with each phrasal verb in part A.

8 CONVERSATION I can't carry a tune.

A Listen and practice.

Emma: Are you going to Lina's party tonight?
Alice: No, I don't think so. I don't really feel up to it.
Emma: You haven't been going out much since you broke up with Carter.
Alice: I guess not. He's friends with all my friends, you know.
Emma: You need to meet new people. Have you thought about joining a running club? You love running.
Alice: I've thought about that, but they meet at 6 A.M. I'm not really a morning person.
Emma: Well . . . maybe you could take part in our singing group. I've made a lot of good friends there.
Alice: Um, I don't think so. Remember when we did karaoke? I can't carry a tune to save my life!
Emma: Yeah, I remember. . . . Well, I guess you'd better get used to waking up early. Just think of all the cute guys who go running in the park in the morning.

B **CLASS ACTIVITY** What are some other good ways to meet people?

9 GRAMMAR FOCUS

Making suggestions

With modals + verbs
Maybe you could take part in a singing group.

With gerunds
What about joining a running club?
Have you thought about asking your friends to introduce you around?

With negative questions
Why don't you do some volunteer work?

With infinitives
One option is to join a club.
It might be a good idea to check out the cultural events at the university.

GRAMMAR PLUS see page 140

A Circle the correct answers. Then practice with a partner.

1. **A:** What can I do to keep up with all my assignments in college?
   B: **Maybe** / **One option** you could stay in on weeknights.
2. **A:** What can I do to get in shape?
   B: **Why don't you** / **Have you thought about** working out at the gym?
3. **A:** How can I save money?
   B: **Why don't you** / **What about** come up with a budget?
4. **A:** How can I learn to dance?
   B: **Have you thought about** / **It might be a good idea** to take dance classes.
5. **A:** How can I build self-confidence?
   B: **What about** / **Why don't you** participating in more social activities?

B **GROUP WORK** Take turns asking and answering the questions in part A. Answer with your own suggestions.

10 LISTENING Resolutions

A Listen to a conversation between three friends on New Year's Eve. Check (✓) the resolution each person makes and write their friends' suggestions.

	New Year's resolutions		Suggestions
1. **Edward**	☐ get a better job	☐ start a project	
2. **Selena**	☐ have more energy	☐ go back to school	
3. **Hannah**	☐ fix her relationship problems	☐ spend more time on social media	

B GROUP WORK Decide on your own suggestion for each person. Then vote as a class on the best suggestions.

11 SPEAKING Breaking a habit

GROUP WORK Make three suggestions for how to break each of these bad habits. Then share your ideas with the class. Which ideas are the most creative?

How can I stop . . . ?

drinking too much soda

biting my nails

spending more money than I can afford

"One thing you could do is carry a bottle of water with you all the time. And why don't you . . . ?"

12 WRITING Sound advice

A Read the posts from a question and answer website. Choose one of the posts below and make a list of suggestions. Then write a reply.

ASK ANYTHING! ? My account

My girlfriend and I argue all the time. We care about each other a lot, but we don't seem to agree about anything. I don't want to break up with her, but I can't put up with this much longer. What can I do?

In: Relationship *Posted: 10 hours ago*

I am 21 years old and a college graduate. My boss never gives me any important work to do, and he says it's because I'm too young. How can I convince him that I'm capable of doing the job?

In: Work and career *Posted: 1 day ago*

B GROUP WORK Take turns reading your advice. Whose advice do you think will work? Why?

13 READING

A Scan the article. Who is the article about? What idea did he have?

Improving the world – one idea at a time

[1] Jack Andraka was 15 when he came up with an idea for a new way to test for pancreatic cancer. When Andraka was 14, a family friend died of the disease, and this affected him deeply. This kind of cancer is particularly lethal because there is no test you can have done to find it in the early stages. By the time standard tests determine you have the disease, it is often too late. Realizing that this was the case, Andraka decided to try to develop a test that might catch problems at the earliest stages.

[2] The road ahead looked difficult for Andraka. He was still a high school student, and he wanted to create something that no one else had done. But Andraka read endlessly about the disease, wrote a proposal for his idea, and sent it out to 200 cancer researchers. Only one professor, Dr. Anirban Maitra, responded positively. Dr. Maitra agreed to work with Andraka on his idea, giving him guidance and access to a laboratory.

[3] The next big reward for Andraka's perseverance was winning the grand prize at the Intel International Science and Engineering Fair. This prestigious award is given to young innovators who have developed a world-changing idea. Developing the test is likely to take many years, but Andraka hopes the test will eventually improve people's lives – and maybe save them.

[4] Jack Andraka is not alone as a young innovator. After all, there were 1,499 other contestants for the Intel award, and all of them had ground-breaking ideas. For Andraka, having a family that loves science and encourages creative thinking gave him an advantage. But the key for Andraka is that reading, research, and discovery are just plain fun – and the chance to improve the world around him in the process makes it even better.

B Read the article. Write the number of each paragraph next to its summary sentence.

______ One doctor's help makes the unlikely become possible.
______ A personal experience creates a groundbreaking idea.
______ Family support and a passion for discovery can lead to great things.
______ Although he won a big prize, there's plenty of work ahead.

C Choose the correct answers.

1. Pancreatic cancer is so serious because **there is no treatment / it is hard to diagnose early**.
2. Andraka was inspired to find a solution by **an upsetting experience / reading about a disease**.
3. The response to Andraka's proposal was **fairly positive / largely negative**.
4. Andraka's test for pancreatic cancer is **in use now / being developed now**.
5. Andraka's family helped him by **encouraging him / working on his idea**.

D **GROUP WORK** If you could come up with an idea to help humanity, what would it be?

10 A matter of time

- Discuss important past events
- Make predictions

1 SNAPSHOT

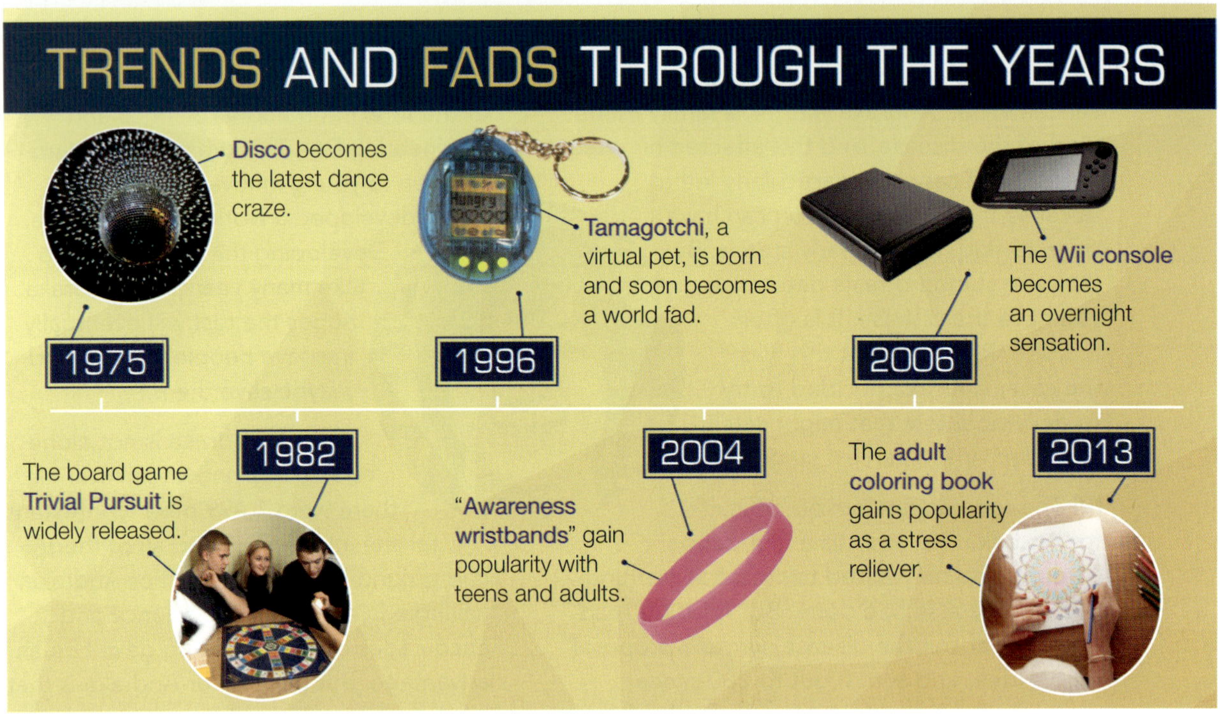

Have any of these fads ever been popular in your country?
Can you think of other fads from the past or present?
Is there anything popular right now that you think is just a fad?

2 PERSPECTIVES Quiz show

A Read the questions from a quiz show. Do you know the answers? Check (✓) your guesses.

1. When was the first home video game console released?
☐ **a.** in 1967 ☐ **b.** in 1972 ☐ **c.** in 1981

2. How long has Washington, D.C., been the capital of the United States?
☐ **a.** since 1776 ☐ **b.** since 1783 ☐ **c.** since 1800

3. How long were the Beatles together?
☐ **a.** for 8 years ☐ **b.** for 10 years ☐ **c.** for 15 years

4. When did World War I take place?
☐ **a.** during the 1910s ☐ **b.** during the 1920s ☐ **c.** during the 1940s

B Now listen and check your answers. What information is the most surprising?

3 GRAMMAR FOCUS

Referring to time in the past

A point or period of time in the past

When was the first video game console released?
During the 1970s. **In** the 1970s. Over 40 years **ago**.

How long were the Beatles together?
From 1960 **to** 1970. **For** 10 years.

A period of time that continues into the present

How long has Washington, D.C. been the capital of the United States?
Since 1800. **For** about 220 years.

GRAMMAR PLUS *see page 141*

A Complete the paragraphs with the **bold** words from the grammar box. Then compare with a partner.

1. The Olympic Games originated in ancient Greece about 3,000 years ______. ______ the eighth century BCE ______ the fourth century CE, the games took place in Olympia. The first modern Olympics were held ______ 1896 in Athens, with male participants from 14 nations. Women have only competed in the Olympics ______ 1900.

2. Although no one knows for sure, it's likely that the Chinese invented ice cream about 4,000 years ______. It was probably brought to Italy ______ the thirteenth century by Marco Polo, but the ice cream we enjoy today was probably created in Italy ______ the seventeenth century and spread through Europe ______ the eighteenth century. ______ that time, different flavors have been created, but vanilla is still America's favorite.

B **GROUP WORK** Write two true and two false statements about world events. Then take turns reading your statements. Others give correct information for the false statements.

A: The United Nations was founded about 50 years ago.
B: That's false. It was founded in 1945, after the end of World War II.

4 PRONUNCIATION Syllable stress

A Listen and practice. Notice which syllable has the main stress in these four- and five-syllable words. Notice the secondary stress.

• ● • ●	● • ● •	• ● • ● •
identify	disadvantage	communication
______	______	______
______	______	______

appreciate
assassination
catastrophe
consideration
conversation
revolution

B Listen to the words in the box. Which syllable has the main stress? Write the words in the correct column in part A.

5 WORD POWER Historic events

A Match each word with the best example. Then compare with a partner.

1. achievement ______
2. assassination ______
3. discovery ______
4. election ______
5. epidemic ______
6. natural disaster ______
7. revolution ______
8. terrorist act ______

a. In 2015, an earthquake hit Nepal and killed over 8,000 people.
b. Fidel Castro established a communist government in Cuba in 1959.
c. In 2015, scientists confirmed the existence of water on Mars.
d. Since the early 1980s, HIV has infected more than 70 million people.
e. Barack Obama became the first African American US president in 2009.
f. John Lennon was killed by a fan on December 8, 1980.
g. In 2003, scientists completed the Human Genome Project.
h. Two men invaded and killed the journalists of the *Charlie Hebdo* newspaper in Paris in 2015.

B **PAIR WORK** Give another example for each kind of event in part A.

"The invention of writing was a very important achievement for humankind."

6 DISCUSSION A major impact

GROUP WORK Choose two or three historic events (an election, an epidemic, an achievement, etc.) that had an impact on your country. Discuss the questions.

What happened (or what was achieved)? When did it happen?
What was the immediate effect on your country? the world? your family?
Did it change things permanently? How is life different now?

"The recent economic crisis has had a major impact on our lives . . ."

7 WRITING A biography

A Find information about a person who has had a major influence on the world or your country. Answer these questions. Then write a biography.

What is this person famous for?
How and when did he or she become famous?
What are his or her important achievements?

MALALA YOUSAFZAI
Activist for Women and Children's Rights

Malala was born in 1997 in Pakistan where she spoke out for girls' right to education. When she was 15, she suffered an attack on her life and almost died. She was flown to England, recovered from her injuries, and continued her fight. When she was 17, she became the youngest winner of the Nobel Peace Prize . . .

B **PAIR WORK** Exchange biographies. What additional details can your partner add?

8 INTERCHANGE 10 History buff

Find out how good you are at history.
Student A, go to Interchange 10A on page 124; Student B, go to Interchange 10B on page 126.

9 CONVERSATION I'll be their first guest!

A Listen and practice.

Hazel: Would you want to spend a vacation in space?

Oscar: No, thanks. I'd rather go to the beach. Would you?

Hazel: Of course I would! I'd stay longer, too. Do you think we'll have colonies on Mars in 20 or 30 years?

Oscar: I don't know. Considering how fast we're destroying Earth, we won't be living here for much longer.

Hazel: I'm serious! You know, international space agencies are investing a lot of money in research to develop more powerful rockets.

Oscar: Well, I guess that within 50 years, we'll have set up a research center on Mars, but not a colony.

Hazel: You're probably right. But I'm sure some company will have built a resort on the moon by then. And I'll be their first guest!

B **CLASS ACTIVITY** Do you think Hazel and Oscar's predictions are correct?

10 GRAMMAR FOCUS

Predicting the future with *will*

Use *will* to predict future events or situations.

We **will spend** vacations in space. We **won't have** colonies on Mars.

Use future continuous to predict ongoing actions.

Human beings **will be living** on another planet. We **won't be living** here.

Use future perfect to predict actions that will be completed by a certain time.

Within 50 years, we **will have set up** a research center on Mars.

By 2050, a company **will have built** a resort on the moon.

GRAMMAR PLUS *see page 141*

A Complete these predictions with the correct verb forms. (More than one answer is possible.) Then compare with a partner.

1. Sometime in the future, buildings ________________ (have) green walls and roof gardens to help retain carbon dioxide.
2. By the end of this century, half of the Amazon rain forest ________________ (be) deforested.
3. In 50 years, the world population ________________ (reach) 9 billion.
4. In the future, most of the population ________________ (live) in cities.
5. Soon, computers ________________ (become) more intelligent than humans.
6. In less than 20 years, scientists ________________ (discover) a cure for cancer, but we ________________ (suffer) from new diseases.

B **GROUP WORK** Discuss each prediction in part A. Do you agree or disagree?

A: Sometime in the future, buildings will have green walls and roof gardens to help retain carbon dioxide. What do you think?

B: Oh, I totally agree. That's also a good way to keep the temperature inside cooler in the summer.

C: I'm not so sure that will happen. Green walls are pretty expensive to maintain.

C **CLASS ACTIVITY** Discuss these questions.

1. What three recently developed technologies will have the greatest impact on our lives in the next 20 years?
2. What are the three most important changes that will have occurred on Earth by 2050?
3. Which three jobs will people *not* be doing in 50 years? Why?

11 LISTENING Not in our lifetime

A Listen to people discuss changes that will affect these topics in the future. Write down two changes for each topic.

	Future changes	
1. crime		
2. space travel		
3. environment		
4. energy		
5. money		

B **PAIR WORK** Which changes do you agree will happen? Which ones would most affect you? Why?

12 DISCUSSION Time will tell.

A Think about your dreams and goals for the future. Write down an idea for each category.

an activity you'd like to try
an experience you'd like to have
a skill you'd like to develop
a city where you would like to live
a job you'd like to have
a person you'd like to meet

B **GROUP WORK** Talk about these questions. Use your ideas from part A.

What do you think you'll be doing a year from now? five years from now?
Do you think you'll still be living in the same city? same country?
What are three things you think you'll have accomplished within the next 10 years?
What are three things you won't have done within the next 10 years?
In what ways do you think you'll have changed by the time you retire?

A: A year from now, I think I'll have a new hobby, like slacklining.

B: I'd like to try that, but I'm more interested in traveling.

C: Me too! I think in five years, I'll be living abroad.

13 READING

A Skim the article. Which sentence below could be another title for the article? Why?

Professionals Who Can Change the Future

An Unhappy View of the Future

Good Guesses About the Future

HOME NEWS ABOUT POPULAR NOW

LOOKING INTO THE FUTURE

Futurists (sometimes called futurologists) are professionals who make predictions about the future of human society, the earth, and even the universe. They study the past and present in order to understand how things change and what factors can alter or interrupt these changes.

Since most people are curious about the future, futurists often try to picture how our lives will be different in a certain year. 2050 is a popular target since it is far enough away to require some speculation, but close enough that many of us will see the changes in our lifetime. Here are some of their predictions.

In the area of technology, computers will be nearly a billion times more powerful than they are today. That means that there will be almost no limit to what you can create, store, and display. Computers will also be small enough to implant in people's brains to improve memory, vision, or even to allow paralyzed people to move again. For those who love shopping or travel, a technology called "immersive telepresence" will allow us to actually feel like we are in two places at the same time, buying things in expensive foreign shops or visiting fascinating tourist destinations while sitting at home.

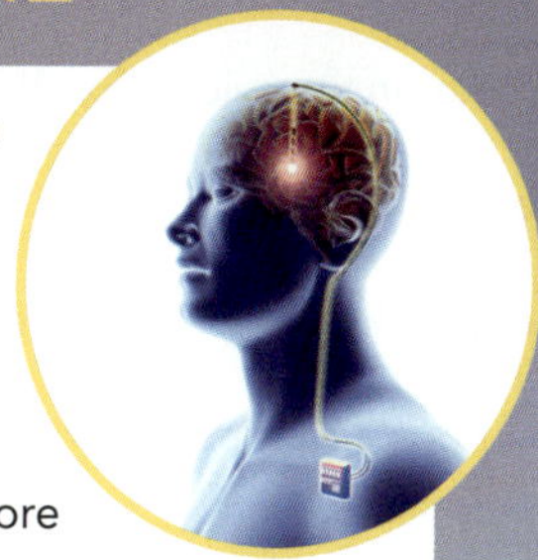

There will be many more people on earth – as many as 9.6 billion. This means that food production and housing will need to increase dramatically. People will live in *mushroom cities*, skyscrapers that house many people and use solar power and other eco-friendly technologies. Futurists also think that – thanks to advances in genetics – we will be close to finding cures for most human diseases. Some futurists even predict that wars and other conflicts will become less common as people learn that they have to get along in order to survive.

Of course, none of these predictions is a certainty. Even futurists can't know how epidemics, natural disasters, or climate change will alter our lives. Having some idea of what is in store for us, however, may help us to make the best choices for our own personal future.

B Read the article. Check (✓) the predictions futurists made about the year 2050.

1. ☐ Computers will be as powerful as they are today.
2. ☐ Tiny computers will help people with physical problems.
3. ☐ Travel will be faster than it is now.
4. ☐ People will be able to explore places without leaving home.
5. ☐ People will need less food.
6. ☐ Many people will live together in eco-friendly buildings.
7. ☐ People will not get sick anymore.
8. ☐ People will fight with each other over food and water.

C **GROUP WORK** Do you agree that the predictions in the article are likely? What changes would you like to see in the future?

Units 9–10 Progress check

SELF-ASSESSMENT

How well can you do these things? Check (✓) the boxes.

I can . . .	Very well	OK	A little
Discuss professional services (Ex. 1)	☐	☐	☐
Give advice and make suggestions (Ex. 2)	☐	☐	☐
Understand and discuss historic events (Ex. 3)	☐	☐	☐
Make predictions about the future (Ex. 4)	☐	☐	☐

1 DISCUSSION Professional services

GROUP WORK Take turns asking questions about these services. When someone answers "yes," find out why and when the service was performed, and who performed it.

have a piece of clothing tailor-made for you
get your carpet cleaned
have your home redecorated or remodeled
get something translated
have your cell phone repaired

A: Have any of you ever had a piece of clothing tailor-made for you?
B: Yes, I have. I had a suit tailor-made when I got married.
C: Really? Why didn't you buy one in a store? . . .

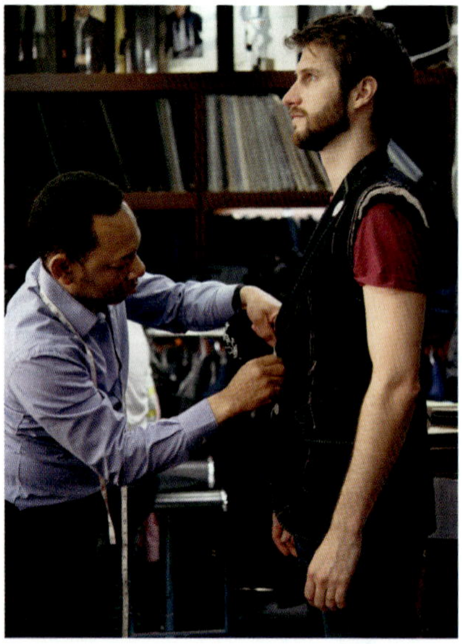

2 ROLE PLAY Advice needed

Student A: Choose one of these problems. Decide on the details of the problem. Then tell your partner about it and get some advice.

I want to move to my own place, but I don't make enough money.
I never have time to do any of the things I enjoy doing. I'm always busy with . . .
I have a job interview in English, and I'm feeling nervous about it.
My in-laws are coming to dinner, but I can't cook at all.

Student B: Your partner tells you about a problem.
Ask questions about it.
Then consider the situation and offer two pieces of advice.

Change roles and choose another situation.

useful expressions

Have you thought about . . . ?
It might be a good idea to . . .
Maybe you could . . .
Why don't you . . . ?

3 LISTENING Important world events

A Listen to people discuss the questions. Write the correct answers.

1. What date did people first land on the moon? ______________
2. When was the first World Cup? ______________
3. When was the Chernobyl disaster? ______________
4. How long did it take to build the *Titanic*? ______________
5. When did the Indian Ocean tsunami occur? ______________

B **PAIR WORK** Which of these events would you like to learn more about? Why?

C **GROUP WORK** Write three more questions about historic events. (Make sure you know the answers.) Then take turns asking your questions. Who has the most correct answers?

4 SURVEY What will happen?

A **CLASS ACTIVITY** How many of your classmates will have done these things in the next 5 years? Write down the number of "yes" and "no" answers. When someone answers "yes," ask follow-up questions.

	"Yes" answers	"No" answers
1. get a (new) job		
2. develop a new skill		
3. move to a new home		
4. learn another language		
5. travel abroad		
6. get a college or master's degree		

A: Five years from now, will you have moved to a new home?
B: Yes, I think I will be living in a new place.
A: Where do you think you'll be living?
B: I'd like to live in a bigger place. Our current apartment is too small.
A: Really? Would you rather live in a house or an apartment?

B **GROUP WORK** Tally the results of the survey as a group. Then take turns telling the class any additional information you found out.

"Most people think they will have moved to a new home. Only three people think they'll be living at their current address. One person thinks she'll be living in a big house in the suburbs, and . . . "

WHAT'S NEXT?

Look at your Self-assessment again. Do you need to review anything?

11 Rites of passage

- Discuss life events and milestones
- Describe regrets and hypothetical situations

1 SNAPSHOT

UNFORGETTABLE FIRSTS

Some moments that matter

- ☐ first sleepover
- ☐ losing your first tooth
- ☐ first day at school
- ☐ first pet
- ☐ first swim in the ocean
- ☐ first crush
- ☐ first trip with friends
- ☐ high school graduation
- ☐ first paycheck
- ☐ getting your driver's license
- ☐ entering college
- ☐ first heartbreak

a sleepover

Which of these first experiences were important for you? Check (✓) them.
How did you feel when you had these experiences?
What other first experiences have you had that you will never forget?

2 CONVERSATION I was so immature.

A Listen and practice.

Jim: Congratulations, graduate! What's next for my favorite nephew?

Luke: I'm your *only* nephew, Uncle Jim!

Jim: But you're still my favorite! Anyway, what *are* your plans?

Luke: I'm looking for a job, so I can make some money before I go to college.

Jim: Ah! After *I* graduated, I went to Alaska to work as a fisherman. It was a tough job, but it helped me grow up.

Luke: How do you mean?

Jim: Until I started working, I'd never had any important responsibilities. I was so immature. But once I moved away from home, I learned to take care of myself.

Luke: So you became independent.

Jim: Yeah, but not for very long, actually. After two months, I moved back home . . . and got a job at your grandfather's store.

Luke: Hey, I think my search just ended. I'm going to talk to Grandpa about a job.

B Listen to the rest of the conversation. What was an important turning point for Jim? for Luke?

3 GRAMMAR FOCUS

Time clauses

Before I graduated from high school, I had never worked.
After I graduated, I went to Alaska to work as a fisherman.
Once I moved away from home, I learned to take care of myself.
The moment I moved away from home, I felt like a different person.
As soon as I got my own bank account, I started to be more responsible.
Until I moved to Alaska, I had never been away from home.
By the time I went to college, I had already lived away from home.

GRAMMAR PLUS see page 142

A Match the clauses in column A with appropriate information in column B. Then compare with a partner.

A	B
1. Until I went to college, ______	**a.** I learned the importance of teamwork.
2. Before I became a parent, ______	**b.** I understood why you shouldn't text and drive.
3. Once I joined a sports team, ______	**c.** I realized that I wasn't a child anymore.
4. The moment I had a car accident, ______	**d.** I learned that love can hurt!
5. As soon as I got my first paycheck, ______	**e.** I had never taken school very seriously.
6. By the time I was 15, ______	**f.** I began to understand the value of money.
7. After I began a relationship, ______	**g.** I had never cooked a real meal.
8. Until I left home, ______	**h.** I had never worried about the future.

B Which of the clauses in column A can you relate to your life? Add your own information to those clauses. Then compare with a partner.

"Until I left home, I had never bought my own clothes."

C **GROUP WORK** What do you think people learn from these events? Write sentences using time clauses in the present. Then take turns reading and talking about them.

1. moving in with roommates
2. buying your own home
3. having a pet
4. getting a credit card
5. getting your first paycheck
6. getting your driver's license
7. getting married
8. becoming a parent

1. *"Once you move in with roommates, you have to learn to work together."*

4 LISTENING Turning points

A Listen to three people describe important events in their lives. Complete the chart.

	Turning point	How it affected him or her
1. Nari		
2. Anthony		
3. Karina		

B Listen again. What do these three people have in common?

C **PAIR WORK** What has been a turning point in your life? Discuss with a partner.

5 SPEAKING Milestones

A **PAIR WORK** In your country, how old are people when these things typically happen?

get a first job
get a driver's license
move out of their parents' home
graduate from college
get married
retire

B **GROUP WORK** Choose three milestones. What do you think life is like before and after each one? Join another pair and discuss.

"Before you get a job, you depend on your family for everything. The moment you get your first paycheck, you . . ."

6 WORD POWER Personal characteristics

A **PAIR WORK** At what age do you think people possess these traits? Check (✓) one or more ages for each trait.

	In their teens	In their 20s	In their 30s	In their 40s	In their 60s
ambitious	☐	☐	☐	☐	☐
argumentative	☐	☐	☐	☐	☐
carefree	☐	☐	☐	☐	☐
dependable	☐	☐	☐	☐	☐
naive	☐	☐	☐	☐	☐
pragmatic	☐	☐	☐	☐	☐
rebellious	☐	☐	☐	☐	☐
sophisticated	☐	☐	☐	☐	☐
wise	☐	☐	☐	☐	☐

B **GROUP WORK** Use the words in part A to describe people you know.
"My mother is dependable. I can always count on her when I need help."

7 PERSPECTIVES That was a mistake.

A Listen to two recent college graduates talk about their regrets. Do you have any similar regrets?

1. I should have done an internship while I was in college.

2. If I'd been more ambitious in college, I could have learned to speak another language.

3. If I hadn't been so irresponsible, I could have gotten better grades.

4. I shouldn't have taken out a student loan to pay for college.

5. If I'd listened to my professors, I would have taken some additional courses.

6. If I hadn't wasted so much money last year, I would have saved enough to start graduate school.

B **GROUP WORK** What advice would you give to these recent grads?

8 GRAMMAR FOCUS

Expressing regret and describing hypothetical situations

Use *should have* + the past participle to express regret.
I **should have done** an internship while I was in college.
I **shouldn't have taken out** a student loan.

Use *would have* + the past participle to express probable outcomes in hypothetical situations.
Use *could have* + the past participle to express possible outcomes.
If I**'d listened** to my professors, I **would have taken** additional courses.
If I **hadn't been** so irresponsible, I **could have gotten** better grades.

GRAMMAR PLUS *see page 142*

A For each statement, write a sentence expressing regret. Then talk with a partner about which statements are true for you.

1. I didn't play any sports when I was younger.
2. I was carefree with money when I was a teenager.
3. I didn't stay in touch with my school friends after I graduated.
4. I was naive when I first started working.
5. I didn't study hard in school.

1. I should have played sports when I was a teenager.

B Match the clauses in column A with appropriate information in column B.

A	B
1. If I hadn't gone to so many parties, ______	**a.** I would have been nicer to my parents.
2. If I'd been more careful, ______	**b.** I wouldn't have borrowed money for a new car.
3. If I'd been wiser, ______	**c.** I would have done better in school.
4. If I'd listened to my financial advisor, ______	**d.** I wouldn't have lost all my documents.
5. If I hadn't been so rebellious, ______	**e.** I wouldn't have argued with my boss.

C Add your own information to the clauses in column A. Then compare in groups.

9 INTERCHANGE 11 Good choices, bad choices

Imagine if things were different. Go to Interchange 11 on page 125.

10 PRONUNCIATION Reduction of *have* and *been*

A Listen and practice. Notice how **have** and **been** are reduced in these sentences.

I should **have been** less selfish when I was younger.
If I'd **been** more ambitious, I could **have** gotten a promotion.

B **PAIR WORK** Complete these sentences and practice them. Pay attention to the reduced forms of **have** and **been**.

I should have been . . . when I was younger.
I should have been . . . in school.
If I'd been more . . ., I could have . . .
If I'd been less . . ., I would have . . .

11 LISTENING My biggest regret

A Listen to a conversation between three friends about regrets. Write two regrets that each person has.

	Regrets	
1. Ariana		
2. Ray		
3. Kira		

B Listen again. Which friend feels differently about regrets? How does he or she feel?

C **PAIR WORK** Do you agree with the attitude about regrets in part B? Why or why not?

12 WRITING An apology

A Think about something you regret doing that you want to apologize for. Consider the questions below. Then write a message of apology.

What did you do? What were the consequences?
Is there any way you can undo those consequences?

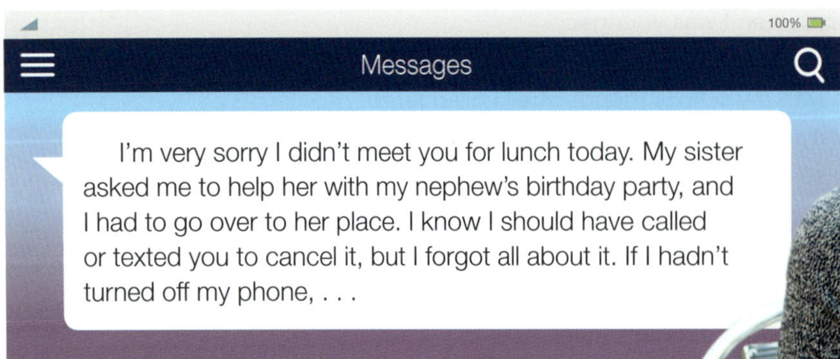

B **PAIR WORK** Read your partner's message. Talk about what you would have done if you'd had a similar regret.

13 READING

A Skim the advice column. What is Paul's problem? What does he ask Stella?

STELLA'S ANSWERS

HOME ABOUT ADVICE ASK STELLA COMMUNITY FOLLOW STELLA

Dear Stella,

I have a problem, and I'm not sure what to do about it. I was studying with my friend Karl, and he let me use his laptop for a minute to look something up. He had been busy typing an essay, so I opened the document again when I was done. But somehow I hit the wrong button, and I deleted the document. All of his work was gone. It was a total accident, and I did say, "Sorry," just so he wouldn't yell at me. But he got really angry and accused me of doing it on purpose. Now Karl is acting really cold towards me, and I can tell he's still angry. It really wasn't my fault, but I still feel bad. Should I apologize anyway just to make him feel better?

Paul in Philadelphia

Dear Paul,

When you've done something that hurt a friend, even by accident, it can be really uncomfortable. You obviously feel bad about deleting Karl's essay, and you didn't mean for it to happen. Unfortunately, it sounds like Karl has a pretty short fuse. Sure, if you'd apologized better at the time, and if you had offered to help him recover his work, it might have smoothed things over. After being accused of sabotage, however, I understand why you didn't apologize again.

What should you do now? First, ask yourself if an apology is necessary. If you don't feel you did anything wrong, it wouldn't mean very much. An apology has to be sincere and heartfelt to be effective. Second, if someone stops treating you like a friend because you made a mistake – which is a form of emotional blackmail – they probably won't believe your apology anyway. Third, a two-way discussion is often more effective than an apology. I think you need to sit down with Karl, tell him how badly you feel, avoid making excuses or trying to blame him, and get on with your friendship. If he still won't forgive you after that, maybe he's not such a great friend after all.

B Read the advice column. Find the words in *italics* in the text. Match the definitions to the words.

1. *short fuse* ______
2. *sabotage* ______
3. *heartfelt* ______
4. *blackmail* ______
5. *forgive* ______

a. act of demanding something from someone in exchange for a benefit
b. quick or violent temper
c. decide not to be angry at someone
d. act of destroying something to get an advantage
e. very sincere

C Check (✓) True, False, or Not given for each statement.

	True	False	Not given
1. The two boys are best friends from childhood.	☐	☐	☐
2. Paul mistakenly deleted some of Karl's work.	☐	☐	☐
3. Karl reacted very calmly at the time.	☐	☐	☐
4. Stella thinks Paul could have improved the situation at the time.	☐	☐	☐
5. Stella believes that both friends need to apologize.	☐	☐	☐
6. Stella thinks even an insincere apology is helpful.	☐	☐	☐
7. Karl's behavior shows that he is not very forgiving.	☐	☐	☐
8. Stella says that Paul and Karl's friendship is over.	☐	☐	☐

D **PAIR WORK** Do you agree with the advice Stella gave Paul? If not, what advice would you give him?

12 Keys to success

- Give personal views and describe qualities for success
- Give reasons

1 SNAPSHOT

HOW SOME MAJOR COMPANIES GOT THEIR NAMES

Nike The company got its name from the ancient Greek goddess of victory.

Google Google comes from *googol*, which is the math term for the number 1 followed by 100 zeros.

Facebook The name was taken from the term for a list with students' names and photos found at American universities.

Samsung In Korean, *sam* means "three" and *sung* means "star," so the name means "three stars." It represents the idea that the company should be everlasting, like stars in the sky.

Skype The original concept for the name was Sky-Peer-to-Peer, which became Skyper, and then Skype.

Häagen-Dazs The name of the American ice cream brand was invented to sound Danish and traditional, but it has no meaning in any language.

Pepsi The soft drink got its name from the word *dyspepsia*, which means indigestion, because its inventor believed it helped treat an upset stomach.

Which of these brands exist in your country? Are they successful?
Do you know the origin of the names of other companies or brands?

2 PERSPECTIVES Business strategies

A Listen to the survey. What makes a business successful? Number the choices from 1 (most important) to 3 (least important).

What makes a business successful?

1. **In order for an app to succeed, it has to be:**
   ☐ easy to use ☐ inexpensive ☐ original
2. **To attract talented professionals, a company should offer:**
   ☐ competitive salaries ☐ flexible working schedules ☐ a good career plan
3. **For a small company to be profitable, it should have:**
   ☐ a good marketing plan ☐ a great product ☐ excellent professionals
4. **To build a successful start-up, it's important to:**
   ☐ have a great product ☐ have a clear business plan ☐ control costs
5. **In order to finance a new business, it's a good idea to:**
   ☐ try a crowd-funding platform ☐ get a bank loan ☐ borrow money from family
6. **For people to work from home, they need to have:**
   ☐ self-discipline ☐ a separate working space ☐ a daily schedule

B **GROUP WORK** Compare your answers. Do you agree on the most important success factors?

3 PRONUNCIATION Reduced words

A Listen and practice. Notice how certain words are reduced in conversation.

In order **før a̸** hotel **tø** be successful, it needs **tø** have friendly service **a̸nd̸** reasonable prices.
Før a̸n entrepreneur **tø** be successful, they have **tø** invest in **a̸** good marketing campaign.

B **PAIR WORK** Take turns reading the sentences in Exercise 2 aloud. Use your first choice to complete each sentence. Pay attention to reduced words.

4 GRAMMAR FOCUS

Describing purpose

Infinitive clauses

To attract talented professionals,	a company should offer competitive salaries.
(**In order**) **to finance** a new business,	it's a good idea to get a bank loan.

Infinitive clauses with *for*

For a small company **to be** profitable,	it should have a good marketing plan.
(**In order**) **for** an app to succeed,	it has to be easy to use.

GRAMMAR PLUS *see page 143*

A Match each goal with a suggestion. Then practice the sentences with a partner. (More than one answer is possible.)

Goals

1. To run a popular convenience store, ______
2. In order to run a profitable clothing boutique, ______
3. To establish a successful language school, ______
4. In order for a health club to succeed, ______
5. For a restaurant to attract more customers, ______

Suggestions

a. it has to offer friendly service.
b. it's a good idea to know the competition.
c. you need to choose the right location.
d. you have to train your staff well.
e. it's important to understand your customers' needs.

B **PAIR WORK** Give another suggestion for each goal in part A.

C **GROUP WORK** What kind of business would you like to have? Talk to your classmates and get suggestions on how to make your business successful.

A: I think I'd like to set up a coffee shop.
B: For a coffee shop to succeed, it's important to choose a good location.
C: And in order to attract customers, you have to offer some tasty desserts, too.

5 WORD POWER Qualities for success

A **PAIR WORK** What qualities are important for success? Rank them from 1 to 5.

A personal trainer	A politician	A news website
☐ athletic	☐ clever	☐ affordable
☐ passionate	☐ charming	☐ attractive
☐ industrious	☐ knowledgeable	☐ entertaining
☐ muscular	☐ persuasive	☐ informative
☐ experienced	☐ tough	☐ well written

B **GROUP WORK** Add one more adjective to each list.

"For a personal trainer to be successful, he or she needs to be . . ."

6 ROLE PLAY The job is yours!

Student A:

Interview two people for one of these jobs. What qualities do they need for success? Decide who is more qualified for the job.

Students B and C:

You are applying for the same job. What are your best qualities? Convince the interviewer that you are more qualified for the job.

sales associate at a trendy boutique   public relations specialist   tour guide

A: To be a good sales associate, you need to be persuasive. Are you?
B: Oh, yes. I'm very good at convincing people. And I'm industrious.
C: I've worked at other stores before, so I'm experienced. And I'm fashionable, too.

7 CONVERSATION It's always packed.

A Listen and practice.

Kyle: What's your favorite club, Lori?
Lori: The Firefly. They have fabulous music, and it's never crowded, so it's easy to get in.
Kyle: That's funny. There's always a long wait outside my favorite club. I like it because it's always packed.
Lori: Why do you think it's so popular?
Kyle: Well, it just opened a few months ago, everything is brand-new and modern, and lots of trendy people go there. It's called the Dizzy Lizard.
Lori: Oh, right! I hear the reason people go there is just to be seen.
Kyle: Exactly! Do you want to go some night?
Lori: I thought you'd never ask!

B **CLASS ACTIVITY** What are some popular places in your city? Do you ever go to any of these places? Why or why not?

8 GRAMMAR FOCUS

Giving reasons

The Firefly is famous **for** its fantastic music.
I like the Dizzy Lizard **because** it's always packed.
Since it's always so packed, there's a long wait outside the club.
It's popular **because of** the trendy people.
Due to the crowds, the Dizzy Lizard is difficult to get into.
The reason (**that/why**) people go there **is** just to be seen.

GRAMMAR PLUS *see page 143*

A Complete the paragraphs with *because, since, because of, for, due to*, and *the reason*. Then compare with a partner. (More than one answer is possible.)

1. Apple is considered one of the most innovative companies in the world. The company is known ______________ introducing original products, but it's also admired ______________ its ability to predict what the market will need in the future. ______________ Apple has been so successful is that it has become a symbol of status and high-end technology.
2. McDonald's is popular worldwide ______________ customers know what to expect when they eat there. Whether you're in Florida or in France, your Big Mac is the same. The company is also known ______________ its ability to adapt to different markets. ______________ the company adjusts some items to local tastes, you can eat a pineapple pie in Thailand or a shrimp burger in Japan.

B **PAIR WORK** Match the situations with the reasons for success. Compare ideas with a partner. Then give two more reasons for each success.

Situation	Reason
1. FedEx is famous _____	**a.** because of its ability to attract new customers.
2. Samsung is a successful company _____	**b.** for its fast and reliable service.
3. Online stores are becoming very popular _____	**c.** for its innovative athletic wear.
4. Netflix has expanded quickly _____	**d.** for its wide selection of products.
5. People buy Levi's jeans _____	**e.** since prices are generally more affordable.
6. Many people like Amazon _____	**f.** due to its high investment in research.
7. Nike is known _____	**g.** since it's advertised worldwide.
8. People everywhere drink Coca-Cola _____	**h.** because they appeal to people of different ages and lifestyles.

A: FedEx is famous for its fast and reliable service.
B: I think another reason why FedEx is famous is . . .

C **GROUP WORK** What are some successful companies in your country? Why are they successful?

9 LISTENING What have you got to lose?

A Listen to radio commercials for three different businesses. What are two special features of each place?

	Fitness For Life	Beauty To Go	Like-New Repair Services
1.			
2.			

B Listen again. Complete the slogan for each business.

1. "Fitness For Life, where ______________________________."
2. "Beauty To Go. When and where you want, beauty ______________________________."
3. "Like-New Repair Services. Don't let your phone ______________________________."

C **GROUP WORK** Which business do you think would be the most successful in your city? Why?

10 INTERCHANGE 12 Advertising taglines

How well do you know the slogans companies use for their products?
Go to Interchange 12 on page 127.

11 DISCUSSION Ads and commercials

GROUP WORK Discuss these questions.

When you watch TV, do you pay attention to the commercials? Why or why not?
When you're online, do you click on any ads that you see?
What ads attract your attention?
What are some effective commercials or ads you remember?
What made them effective?
What is the funniest commercial you've ever seen? the worst? the most shocking?
Which celebrities have been in commercials or ads?
Has this affected your opinion of the product?
Has it affected your opinion of the celebrity?

12 WRITING A commercial

A Choose one of your favorite products. Read the questions and make notes about the best way to sell it. Then write a one-minute TV or online commercial.

What's good or unique about the product?
Why would someone want to buy or use it?
Can you think of a clever name or slogan?

Do you want a car that is dependable and economical? Do you need more space for your family? The new Genius SUV has it all. Genius offers the latest safety technologies and . . .

B **GROUP WORK** Take turns presenting your commercials. What is good about each one? Can you give any suggestions to improve them?

13 READING

A Scan the article. What does "sticky" mean in the advertising world?

BRAIN INVASION:

WHY WE CAN'T FORGET SOME ADS

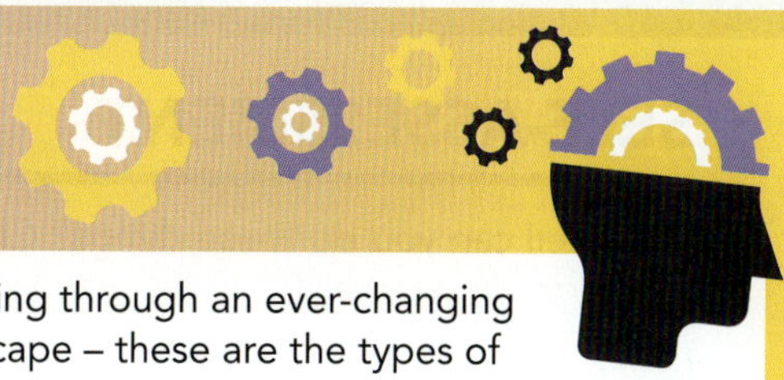

Advertisements: They're all over our social media pages; they arrive as text messages; they interrupt our favorite shows; and they bombard us in the streets. In order to survive the constant barrage of advertising, we learn to ignore most of what we see. But what is it that makes certain ads "sticky"? In other words, why do we remember some ads while managing to completely forget others?

According to advertising experts, an ad needs three key elements to make it unforgettable. In the first place, it needs to be clear and simple. TV commercials usually last about 30 seconds, so a complicated or confusing presentation will not do the job. For an ad to be "sticky," it has to be obvious enough that we can pick up the message in a split second.

More importantly, ads should appeal to our senses and emotions. When we really feel something, it tends to stick in our brains much longer than if we simply understand it. This is the reason why so much advertising depends on emotional music and images of family, romance, or success that relate directly to our own hopes and dreams.

One more element necessary to make an ad successful is surprise. When we see something out of the ordinary, it makes us take notice whether we want to or not. A talking animal, a beautifully dressed model diving into a swimming pool, a car zooming through an ever-changing landscape – these are the types of things that grab our attention.

But do "sticky" ads actually make us buy the products? That's another story. Sometimes the most memorable ads make people laugh or mention them to their friends, but they don't actually convince people to buy anything. Still, after watching a "sticky" ad, we usually remember the name of the company it promotes. And in a world with so many brands and products, that is almost as important as sales.

B Read the article. Check (✓) the three things that make an ad memorable.

- ☐ an uncomplicated concept
- ☐ a puzzle or mystery
- ☐ a short time span
- ☐ a sensual or emotional appeal
- ☐ a familiar scene or situation
- ☐ something unexpected or strange

C Read these descriptions of two ads. According to the article, are these "sticky" ads? Explain why.

A family of four is having breakfast together, and they're all looking tired. The father pours each of them a glass of "Super Juice," and as they all drink it, they are transformed into costumed superheroes. As they leave, the mother says, "Ready to save the world, team?"

A young couple are in a luxurious car; the woman is driving. They are driving quickly through lush countryside. They glance at other and smile. A voiceover says: "The Eternity: a car that feels like home."

D **PAIR WORK** Describe an advertisement that has stuck in your mind. Why do you think you remember it? Has it influenced what you buy in any way?

Units 11–12 Progress check

SELF-ASSESSMENT

How well can you do these things? Check (✓) the boxes.

I can . . .	Very well	OK	A little
Describe important life events and their consequences (Ex. 1)	☐	☐	☐
Describe and explain regrets about the past (Ex. 2)	☐	☐	☐
Describe hypothetical situations in the past (Ex. 2)	☐	☐	☐
Understand and give reasons for success (Ex. 3, 4)	☐	☐	☐
Give reasons (Ex. 4)	☐	☐	☐

1 SPEAKING Important events

A What are two important events for each of these age groups? Complete the chart.

Children	Teenagers	People in their 20s	People in their 40s

B **GROUP WORK** Talk about the events. Why is each event important? What do people learn from each event?

A: Learning to drive is an important event for teenagers.
B: Why is learning to drive an important milestone?
A: Once they learn to drive, . . .

useful expressions

after
as soon as
the moment
by the time
once
before
until

2 GAME Regrets

A Write three regrets you have about the past.

1. *I wish I hadn't argued with my boss.*

B **GROUP WORK** What if the situations were different? Take turns. One student expresses a regret. The next student adds a hypothetical result, and so on, for as long as you can.

A: I shouldn't have argued with my boss.
B: If you hadn't argued with your boss, she wouldn't have fired you.
C: If she hadn't fired you, you could have . . .

3 LISTENING The road to success

A Listen to a career coach discuss some factors necessary to work for yourself. Write down the three factors that you hear.

	Factor	Why is it important?
1.		
2.		
3.		

B Listen again. In your own words, write why each factor is important.

C **PAIR WORK** If you could work for yourself, what would you do? Why?

4 DISCUSSION Effective strategies

A **PAIR WORK** Choose two businesses and discuss what they need to be successful. Then write three sentences describing the most important factors.

- ☐ a convenience store
- ☐ a gourmet supermarket
- ☐ a dance club
- ☐ a beach hotel
- ☐ a juice bar
- ☐ a used clothing store

In order for a convenience store to be successful, it has to be open 24 hours.

B **GROUP WORK** Join another pair. Share your ideas. Do they agree?

A: We think in order for a convenience store to be successful, it has to be open 24 hours.

B: Really? But many convenience stores close at midnight.

C **GROUP WORK** Now choose a popular business that you know about. What are the reasons for its success?

"I think Mark's Comics is successful because their comic books are affordable and they don't mind if people hang out there and read."

useful expressions

It's successful because (of) . . .
It's popular due to . . .
The reason it's successful is . . .
It's become popular since . . .
It's famous for . . .

WHAT'S NEXT?

Look at your Self-assessment again. Do you need to review anything?

13 What might have been

- Suggest explanations and reasons
- Give opinions and advice about past situations

1 SNAPSHOT

PET PEEVES

IT DRIVES ME CRAZY WHEN . . .

- people push too close to me on the subway.
- someone borrows my things without asking.
- people keep interrupting me.
- a couple starts arguing in public.
- people don't pay for their share at a restaurant.
- a friend criticizes another friend.
- someone is late for no reason.
- people chew with their mouths open.
- a friend constantly asks me for favors.
- someone cuts in line in front of me.

Which of the pet peeves do you have about people you know? Which one is the worst?
What other pet peeves do you have?
Do you do any of these things? When and why?

2 CONVERSATION He might have gone out.

A Listen and practice.

Chris: Didn't Tyler ask us to come at 7:30?
Ava: Yes, and it's almost 8:00 now. Why don't we ring the bell again? He must not have heard it.
Chris: That's impossible. We've been ringing the bell for more than 10 minutes.
Ava: He must have fallen asleep. You know Tyler has been working so hard on his new project.
Chris: Or he might have forgotten about our dinner and just gone out.
Ava: No, he couldn't have forgotten. I just talked to him about it this morning. Besides, the lights are on. He could have had an emergency. He might not have had time to call us.
Chris: Yeah, maybe. I'll call him and find out.
Ava: And?
Chris: He's not answering. . . . Now *I'm* getting worried.

B Listen to the rest of the conversation. What happened?

3 PRONUNCIATION Reduction in past modals

A Listen and practice. Notice how **have** is reduced in these sentences.

He may **have** fallen asleep. She might **have** gone out.

B Listen and practice. Notice that **not** is not contracted or reduced in these sentences.

He might **not** have had time to call us. She must **not** have heard the doorbell.

4 GRAMMAR FOCUS

Past modals for degrees of certainty

It's almost certain.

He **must have fallen** asleep.

He **must not have heard** the doorbell.

It's not possible.

He **couldn't have forgotten** about it.

It's possible.

He **may/might have gone out**.

He **may/might not have had** time to call us.

He **could have had** an emergency.

GRAMMAR PLUS *see page 144*

A Read each situation and choose the best explanation. Then practice with a partner. (Pay attention to the reduced forms in past modals.)

Situation	Explanation
1. Marcia seems very relaxed. ______	**a.** She must have gotten fired.
2. Claire is packing her things. ______	**b.** He might have worked late last night.
3. Jeff got a bad grade on his test. ______	**c.** She may have just come back from vacation.
4. Rodrigo looks very tired today. ______	**d.** He couldn't have heard good news.
5. Julia didn't talk to her friends in the cafeteria. ______	**e.** He might not have studied very hard.
6. Ahmed got a call and looked worried. ______	**f.** She must not have seen them.

B PAIR WORK Suggest different explanations for each situation in part A.

5 LISTENING What could have happened?

A GROUP WORK Look at the pictures. What do you think happened? Offer an explanation for each event.

1

2

B Listen to the explanations for the two events in part A and take notes. What *did* happen? How similar were your explanations?

6 SPEAKING What's your guess?

A **PAIR WORK** What do you think were the reasons for these events? Suggest two different explanations for each.

1. The bride didn't show up for her wedding. She sent a bunch of flowers to the groom with a note: "Thank you."
2. A man arrived at the airport with a suitcase and saw his brother. He grabbed a cab and went back home.
3. It was a hot, sunny day. A man arrived home. He was soaking wet.

B **GROUP WORK** Each student thinks of two situations like the ones in part A. Others suggest explanations.

A: A man went around town and bought all the copies of the latest issue of a specific magazine.

B: Well, the magazine might have had an article about him.

7 INTERCHANGE 13 Think of the possibilities!

What's your best explanation for some unusual events? Go to Interchange 13 on page 128.

8 PERSPECTIVES I'm going nuts!

A Listen to a person complaining about her family members. Check (✓) the response you think is best for each problem.

Last night, my sister borrowed my car without asking. She did call me a couple of times, but I was in a meeting and couldn't answer the phone. We had a big fight, and now we're not speaking.

- [ ] She shouldn't have used your car without permission, no matter what.
- [ ] You could have been more understanding. After all, she tried to call you first.

My nephew is so inconsiderate. He called me at 3:00 in the morning to talk about his problems with his best friend, and I had to get up very early to work. I was really mad.

- [ ] You could have told him that you had to get up early the next day.
- [ ] Your nephew is always doing that. You shouldn't have answered his call.

My brother came over for the weekend with his wife and three kids. They made such a mess of the apartment! I'll never invite them over again.

- [ ] I would have asked them to help clean up the place.
- [ ] I wouldn't have invited them to spend the weekend. Having overnight guests can be really stressful.

B Do you talk about pet peeves with your friends? Do they give you advice?

9 GRAMMAR FOCUS

Past modals for judgments and suggestions

Judging past actions

You **should have asked** your sister to help.

He **shouldn't have used** your car.

Suggesting alternative past actions

You **could have told** her that you had to get up early.

I **would have asked** them to help clean up the place.

I **wouldn't have invited** them to spend the weekend.

GRAMMAR PLUS *see page 144*

A Complete the conversations using past modals with the verbs given. Then practice with a partner.

1. **A:** My boss asked me to help her choose a gift for her husband, and I ended up spending all day at the mall.
   B: You ______________ (make up) an excuse not to help her. She ______________ (not ask) for such a personal favor in the first place.
2. **A:** I lent my sister-in-law some money a year ago, and she never paid it back.
   B: She ______________ (pay) it back already! Well, I ______________ (not lend) money to her anyway. I never lend money to relatives.
3. **A:** Austin invited me out to dinner, but when the check came, he said he was broke!
   B: I ______________ (not pay) for him. I ______________ (tell) him to wash the dishes. He ______________ (not invite) you if he didn't have enough money.
4. **A:** I can't believe my cousin came over and stayed until 1:00 in the morning!
   B: He ______________ (not stay) so late. You ______________ (start) yawning. Maybe he would have gotten the hint!

B **PAIR WORK** Think of another suggestion or comment for each situation above.

10 WORD POWER Reactions

A Helena's boyfriend forgot their anniversary. How does she react? Match each reaction with the best example.

Reaction	Example
1. an assumption _____	**a.** "Sometimes you're so selfish."
2. a criticism _____	**b.** "You could take me out to dinner."
3. a demand _____	**c.** "You must have wanted to break up with me."
4. an excuse _____	**d.** "I bet you went out with your friends."
5. a prediction _____	**e.** "Now you'll have to get me a really nice gift."
6. a suggestion _____	**f.** "I know you've been busy lately. It just slipped your mind."
7. a suspicion _____	**g.** "If you ever forget another important date, I'll never talk to you again."
8. a warning _____	**h.** "You'll probably forget my birthday, too!"

B **GROUP WORK** Imagine that someone was late for class, or choose another situation. Give an example of each reaction in the list above.

11 LISTENING What should they have done?

A Listen to descriptions of three situations. What would have been the best thing to do in each situation? Check (✓) the best suggestion.

1. ☐ Simon should have kept the ring for himself.
   ☐ He should have called the police.
   ☐ He did the right thing.
2. ☐ Jana shouldn't have mentioned her last job at all in her application.
   ☐ She should have been honest in her application and admitted she made a mistake.
   ☐ She did the right thing.
3. ☐ Martin should have reported what his boss did as soon as he found out.
   ☐ He should have withdrawn more money and blamed it on his boss.
   ☐ He did the right thing.

B **PAIR WORK** What would you have done in each situation in part A?

12 DISCUSSION How would you have reacted?

GROUP WORK Read each situation. Say what the person could have or should have done, and what you would have done.

"It was my friend's birthday, and he had invited a few close friends out to celebrate. I forgot all about it, so I called him the next day and pretended I'd had to take my mother to the hospital." – Warren

"My sister got a new haircut, and I thought it looked a little dated. I didn't want to hurt her feelings, so I told her I liked it." – Sonia

"I didn't have any money to buy my cousin a birthday present, so I gave her something I had received previously as a gift. My brother told my cousin about my regifting, and now she's mad at me." – Chase

"I went to my in-laws' house for dinner last night. My husband thinks his mother is a great cook, but the food was awful! I didn't know what else to do, so I ate it." – Fay

A: Warren should have told his friend the truth.
B: I agree. He could have taken his friend out to make up for it.
C: I think I would have . . .

13 WRITING A tricky problem

A Think of a complicated situation from your own experience. Write a paragraph describing the situation, but don't explain how you resolved it.

> *I have a close friend who doesn't get along with my other friends. He's a nice guy, friendly and funny, but every time we all go out, he makes a fuss over how much everyone should pay. Last week, my friends were going to dinner, and he wanted to come along. I didn't want to hurt his feelings . . .*

B **PAIR WORK** Exchange papers. Write a short paragraph about how you would have resolved your partner's situation.

C **PAIR WORK** Read your partner's resolution to your situation. Tell your partner how you resolved it. Whose resolution was better?

14 READING

A Skim the article. What do the two unexplained events have in common?

Messages from Outer Space, or a Leaking Pipe?

Home | Sciencenews | Technology | Articles | Blog | Community

Even though we know so much about the world around us, unexplained events still take place. Read about these two events. What do you think may have happened?

Since 2008, people around the world have been reporting a mysterious sound that seems to come from the sky. Some people say it sounds like trumpets playing. Others say it is like sound effects from sci-fi movies. The phenomenon has caused both fear and fascination, and many people have been looking for explanations. One popular idea is that the sound is an announcement of the end of the world, and another

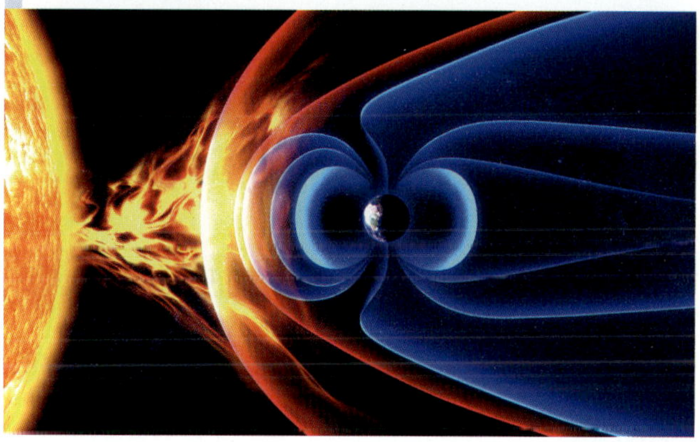

suggests that it's the sound of spaceships. But there may be a more scientific explanation. It involves flares from the sun and energy from the center of the earth. Which explanation do you think might be right?

Of course, there are some strange events that still baffle both the general public and experts. Take the high-pitched noise that has been driving people crazy in Forest Grove, Oregon. To some people, it sounds like a giant flute being played very badly, and to others, it sounds like a train slowing down or truck brakes squealing. The sound is coming from under the street, but gas, water, and sewer inspectors have said there is nothing wrong down there. One resident was so sure it was a serious gas leak that he was ready to flee. However, experts say that a leak would make a different sound, and people would definitely smell gas. How would you explain this mysterious and annoying event?

B Read the article. Then answer the questions.

1. To what two things have people compared the first sound?
2. What non-scientific explanations have been offered?
3. What sort of sound are people in Forest Grove hearing?
4. What explanation has been proven untrue?
5. If there had been a gas leak, what would be different?

C Which of these statements are facts? Which are opinions? Check (✓) Fact or Opinion.

	Fact	Opinion
1. Science has not explained everything that happens.	☐	☐
2. Some sounds mean the end of the world is coming.	☐	☐
3. The first sound is caused by energy from planets.	☐	☐
4. The sound in Forest Grove is very annoying.	☐	☐
5. The Forest Grove sound comes from under the street.	☐	☐
6. Gas lines and other systems in Forest Grove have no problems.	☐	☐
7. No local problems can explain the Forest Grove noise.	☐	☐

D PAIR WORK Which explanations of the events in the article do you think are the most likely? least likely? Can you think of any other possible explanations?

14 Creative careers

- Describe steps in a process
- Discuss jobs in entertainment and the media

1 SNAPSHOT

MILESTONES IN CONTEMPORARY CINEMATOGRAPHY

THE FIRST . . .

- movie with **Dolby Digital** sound. – *Batman Returns* (1992)
- **computer-animated** feature film. – *Toy Story* (1995)
- major movie **shot entirely in digital video**. – *Star Wars Episode II: Attack of the Clones* (2002)
- computer-animated **motion-captured** film. – *The Polar Express* (2004)
- movie to be **released simultaneously** in theaters, on DVD, and on the Internet. – *EMR* (2005)
- **film directed by a woman** to win the Oscar for Best Picture. – *The Hurt Locker* (2008)
- full-length feature film **shot on a phone**. – *Olive* (2011)
- major movie **filmed at 48 frames per second**, instead of the standard 24 fps. – *The Hobbit: An Unexpected Journey* (2012)

Have you seen any of these movies? Did you enjoy them?
What's the most popular movie playing right now? Have you seen it? Do you plan to?
Are there many movies made in your country? Name a few of your favorites.

2 CONVERSATION I have more control.

A Listen and practice.

Clara: Thanks for coming to the film festival! Directing this film was amazing, and I'm happy to answer your questions about it.
Diego: Yes, hi. What is it like to direct an animated movie? Is it different from live action?
Clara: Well, for one thing, I have a lot more control. There are no actors to argue with me!
Diego: I guess not! But how do you direct cartoon characters?
Clara: Well, after a screenplay is chosen, many drawings of the characters are presented to me . . .
Diego: And you get to choose which ones to use?
Clara: Even better: I can change them if I want. The characters have to be drawn just right – like I see them in my mind.
Diego: So you decide a lot about the characters early on.
Clara: Definitely. By the time the voice actors are picked, the characters feel like old friends!

B Listen to the rest of the conversation. Who helps Clara choose the voice actors?

3 GRAMMAR FOCUS

The passive to describe process

***is/are* + past participle**	**Modal + *be* + past participle**
A screenplay **is chosen**.	The characters **have to be drawn** just right.
Many drawings **are presented**.	The drawings **might be changed** 10 times.

GRAMMAR PLUS *see page 145*

A The sentences below describe how an animated movie is made. First, complete the sentences using the passive. Then compare with a partner.

Storyboard and animation steps

1. First, storyboards ________________ (draw) by story artists. For some movies, over 200,000 storyboards might ________________ (draw).
2. Next, the storyboards need to ________________ (place) in order.
3. After the storyboarding process ________________ (complete), technical directors must ________________ (hire).
4. Then, the scenes and characters have to ________________ (create) on the computer by the technical directors.
5. Finally, movement ________________ (add) to the scenes by animators. In addition, the scenes ________________ (populate) with background characters.

Voice-over steps

6. First, temporary "scratch" voices ________________ (record). Sometimes scratch voices are so good that they ________________ (not replace).
7. Later, professional actors ________________ (hire) to record the character voices. For some movies, studios hire famous actors so their names can ________________ (use) as a marketing tool.
8. The lines ________________ (rehearse) and the same line ________________ (record) in different ways.
9. Finally, the best recording ________________ (choose) for the final movie.

B **PAIR WORK** What are some steps that happen after the animated movie is complete? Discuss with a partner.

"After all that, the movie is sent to theaters."

4 LISTENING It was too predictable.

A Listen to Casey and Grant talk about things that often happen in movies. Number the parts of a movie in the order they are mentioned.

	Movie example
☐ A new plan is put into action.	*Luke planned to destroy the Death Star.*
☐ A problem is presented.	
☐ Something bad happens, and all hope is lost.	
☐ The main character is introduced.	
☐ The bad guy is defeated.	

B Listen again. For each movie part above, write an example from the movies the friends discuss.

5 SPEAKING Tutorials

A PAIR WORK What do you think is required to make a short movie? Put the pictures in order and describe the steps. More than one order may be possible. Use the vocabulary to help you.

[ ] add titles and credits

[ ] rehearse the lines

[ ] shoot the movie

[ ] find a location

[ ] edit the movie

[1] write the script

A: Making a short movie requires many steps. First, the script needs to be written.
B: Right! And after that, a location must be found.
A: I agree. Then . . .

B PAIR WORK Choose one of these topics. Come up with as many steps as you can.

preparing a school party	organizing a fundraising campaign	developing a mobile app
organizing a trip abroad	planning a wedding	putting on a school musical

C GROUP WORK Share your information from part B with another pair.

6 WRITING Describing a process

A Write about one of the topics from Exercise 5, part B or use your own idea. Describe the different steps in the process.

Developing a mobile app requires a lot of work. First, the objective of the app must be defined. Then, a prototype should be built. After that, the prototype can be tested by potential users or friends. Then a developer needs to be hired, and . . .

B PAIR WORK Read your partner's description. Can you think of any more steps?

7 WORD POWER Creative jobs

A What kind of jobs are these? Complete the chart with the compound nouns. (More than one answer is possible.)

band manager	game animator	songwriter	talk show host
club DJ	gameplay programmer	storyboard artist	quality assurance analyst
editorial director	news photographer	stunt person	web content manager

Film/TV jobs	Publishing jobs	Gaming jobs	Music jobs

B **GROUP WORK** Choose four jobs from part A. Describe each job.

"A band manager negotiates contracts for artists and helps promote their careers."

8 PERSPECTIVES Career questions

A Listen to the career questions that people have. How would you answer them?

I have a degree in journalism, and I'm an amateur photographer. I'm considering a career as a news photographer who covers conflicts around the world. Do you think that's too dangerous?

Videographers like me, who shoot weddings and other social events, often work evenings and weekends. I want to have a nine-to-five job, so I'm looking for a job with a major studio. Is that a good move?

I love movies and I love action, so I'm thinking of becoming a stunt person – you know, the person who takes the place of an actor in dangerous scenes. What do you think?

A talk show host, who interviews artists, politicians, and celebrities, gets to meet lots of people. I love to meet new people. Do you think that would be a good job for me?

B **PAIR WORK** Which of these careers do you think would be the most interesting? Why?

9 PRONUNCIATION Review of stress in compound nouns

A Listen and practice. Notice how the first word in a compound noun usually receives greater stress.

band manager   talk show host   game animator   news photographer   stunt person

B Practice the sentences in Exercise 8. Pay attention to the word stress in the compound nouns.

10 GRAMMAR FOCUS

Defining and non-defining relative clauses

Defining relative clauses are used to identify people.

I want to become a photographer. I want to cover conflicts. → I want to become a photographer **who/that covers conflicts**.

Non-defining relative clauses give further information about people.

Videographers shoot weddings and social events. They work evenings and weekends. → Videographers, **who shoot weddings and social events**, work evenings and weekends.

GRAMMAR PLUS *see page 145*

A Do these sentences contain defining (**D**) or non-defining (**ND**) clauses? Write **D** or **ND**. Add commas to the non-defining clauses. Then compare with a partner.

1. The art editor who creates the look of a magazine should make it attractive. ______
2. A game programmer is the person who writes the computer code that runs and controls a game. ______
3. The extras are the people who appear in the background scenes. ______
4. The producer who is responsible for the budget is the big boss in an animation studio. ______

B Add the non-defining relative clauses in parentheses to the sentences.

1. A game designer works closely with the programmers. (who creates new games)

   ____

   ____

2. A lead vocalist is the main voice on stage. (who may also be a songwriter)

   ____

   ____

3. A news reporter collects information about news and events. (who should be impartial)

   ____

   ____

4. A photo editor selects the photos that go into magazines. (who is responsible for the quality and content of images)

   ____

   ____

C Write three sentences with relative clauses about jobs you know. Compare with a partner.

11 INTERCHANGE 14 Celebrities

Can you guess who the celebrities are? Go to Interchange 14 on page 129.

READING

A Scan the title and first paragraph of the article. Who do you think it was written for? Why?

Home | News | Entertainment | Articles | Blog | Community

THE TRUTH ABOUT BEING A FILM EXTRA

by Anna Murphy

When people discover that I work as a film and TV extra, they always ask me the same questions: *Is it easy to get work? Isn't it boring? Do you get to meet famous actors? Does it pay well?* My answers are pretty standard as well: yes, sometimes, once in a while, and . . . kind of. The life of an extra is both more interesting and more boring than you might imagine.

Extras, who play the people in crowds, on streets, or in the background of indoor scenes, can come from all walks of life. Unlike many extras, I'm a trained actor. I do get real speaking roles, but work can be hard to come by if you're not an in-demand star. I'm registered with an agency that deals exclusively with extras, so I get calls all the time. The agency explains who I'll be – someone in a crowd, a member of a jury, a clerk – and tells me where to go. Call time is usually bright and early, so I try to get to bed at a reasonable hour.

Sometimes being an extra is a "hurry up and wait" job. In my first extra role, I was one of a group of office workers who come out of a building just as a car explodes in the street. We waited for hours for the scene to be shot, and then went in and out of the building about fifty times, trying to act horrified by a nonexistent explosion. Then we had lunch, changed clothes, and spent the afternoon as customers in a department store.

It may sound like I don't enjoy the work, but I do. Being part of the background in a convincing way is challenging, and being on a film or TV set is always fascinating. A lot of famous actors don't even notice the extras, but the ones who do make the job a lot of fun for everyone. As for the money, it's nothing compared to what the big actors make, but it pretty much pays the bills. And, as a bonus, I've beaten my high scores on all my phone games, thanks to all the time I spend sitting around, waiting for something to happen.

B Read the article. Underline a sentence in the article that answers each question below.

1. What training has the writer had?
2. How does she get work as an extra?
3. What was her first role as an extra?
4. What unexpected advantage of the work does she mention?

C Find words or phrases in the article that mean the same as the following.

1. have very different jobs and life experiences ________________
2. wanted or needed by many people ________________
3. first thing in the morning ________________
4. imaginary ________________
5. difficult ________________

D **PAIR WORK** What job would you most like to have on a film or TV show? Why?

Units 13–14 Progress check

SELF-ASSESSMENT

How well can you do these things? Check (✓) the boxes.

I can . . .	Very well	OK	A little
Speculate about past events (Ex. 1)	☐	☐	☐
Give opinions and advice about past events (Ex. 2)	☐	☐	☐
Describe steps in processes (Ex. 3)	☐	☐	☐
Use relative clauses to give information about people (Ex. 4)	☐	☐	☐

1 LISTENING Something's not right.

A Listen to three conversations. Where do you think each conversation takes place? What do you think might have happened? Take notes.

	Location	What might've happened	What could've happened next
1.			
2.			
3.			

B **PAIR WORK** Decide what happened with your partner. Then decide what could have happened next in each situation. Complete the chart.

2 DISCUSSION Bad moves

A **PAIR WORK** React to these situations. First, make a judgment or suggestion using a past modal. Then add another statement using the reaction in parentheses.

1. Samantha didn't get to work on time today. (a suggestion)
2. Pat took a vacation, and now he doesn't have money for rent. (a warning)
3. Jim didn't study for the test, but he got all the answers correct. (a suspicion)
4. Nick was driving too fast, and the police stopped him. (an excuse)
5. Carl spent the night playing his favorite game online. (a prediction)

"Samantha should have left home earlier. She could have set an alarm."

B **GROUP WORK** Join another pair and compare your comments. Who has the most interesting reaction to each situation?

3 GAME Step by step

A GROUP WORK Look at these topics. Set a time limit. Talk with your group and write as many steps as you can between the first and last parts of each process.

making a grilled cheese sandwich

First, the bread has to be sliced.

____

____

____

____

____

Finally, the sandwich is served on a plate.

organizing a party

First, the guests have to be chosen.

____

____

____

____

____

Finally, the guests are welcomed.

B CLASS ACTIVITY Compare your answers. Which group has the most steps?

4 SPEAKING Your social circle

A Complete these statements about people in your life.

My best friend is a person who ____________________ .

My neighbor, who ____________________ , always ____________________ .

My mother is someone that ____________________ .

My teacher, who ____________________ , is ____________________ .

____________________ is a ____________________ who ____________________ .

B PAIR WORK Compare your answers. Ask two follow-up questions about each of your partner's statements.

A: My best friend is a person who always listens to me when I have a problem.
B: Does she give you good advice?

WHAT'S NEXT?

Look at your Self-assessment again. Do you need to review anything?

15 A law must be passed!

- ▸ Make recommendations about social issues
- ▸ Give opinions about laws and social issues

1 SNAPSHOT

8 UNUSUAL LAWS FROM AROUND THE WORLD

1. A law prohibits unmarried women from parachuting on Sunday in Florida.
2. In Switzerland, it's illegal to keep only one pet if it's a social animal.
3. It's against the law to feed the pigeons in Venice.
4. In some states in Australia, you may not leave the car keys inside an unattended vehicle.
5. In the U.K., women aren't allowed to eat chocolate on public transportation.
6. Businesses must provide rails for tying up horses in Canada.
7. In the state of Washington, it's illegal to pretend your parents are rich.
8. In Finland, taxi drivers must pay royalties if they play music for customers.

Adapted from www.dumblaws.com

Which of these laws would you like to have in your city or country? Why?
Can you think of reasons for these laws?
Do you know of any other unusual laws?

2 PERSPECTIVES Rules and regulations

A Listen to people make recommendations at a city council meeting. Would you agree with these proposals if they were made in your community? Check (✓) your opinion.

CITY OF BRISTOL

MEETING NOTES	STRONGLY AGREE	SOMEWHAT AGREE	DISAGREE
1. Clubs should be required to install soundproof walls.	☐	☐	☐
2. Riding a bike on the sidewalk mustn't be permitted.	☐	☐	☐
3. Pet owners shouldn't be allowed to walk dogs without a leash.	☐	☐	☐
4. Something has got to be done about littering.	☐	☐	☐
5. A law must be passed to control the pollution from vehicles.	☐	☐	☐
6. Children ought to be required to wear a helmet when riding a bike.	☐	☐	☐
7. Schools should only be permitted to serve organic food.	☐	☐	☐

B GROUP WORK Compare your opinions. Try to get your classmates to agree with you.

3 GRAMMAR FOCUS

Giving recommendations and opinions

When you think something is a good idea

Clubs **should be required** to install soundproof walls.

Pet owners **shouldn't be allowed** to walk dogs without a leash.

People **ought (not) to be required** to wear a helmet when riding a bike.

When you think something is absolutely necessary

A law **must be passed** to control the pollution from vehicles.

Riding a bike on the sidewalk **mustn't be permitted**.

A rule **has to be made** to require bike lanes on city streets.

Something **has got to be done** to stop littering.

GRAMMAR PLUS *see page 146*

A Complete the sentences positively or negatively. Choose a modal that shows how strongly you feel about these issues.

1. Young people ____________________ (permit) to vote before age 21.
2. Laws ____________________ (pass) to protect people's online privacy.
3. People ____________________ (allow) to use offensive language in social media.
4. Governments ____________________ (require) to provide health care to all their citizens.
5. Children ____________________ (allow) to play violent video games.
6. Scientists ____________________ (permit) to use animals for research.
7. The sale of fur products ____________________ (prohibit).
8. Something ____________________ (do) to stop the pollution of rivers and oceans.

B **GROUP WORK** Compare your statements. Do you agree with one another? If not, why not?

A: Young people shouldn't be permitted to vote before age 21. They're not prepared.
B: You may have a point, but they could be better informed.
C: Maybe, but in my opinion, . . .

4 DISCUSSION Controversial topics

A **GROUP WORK** Think of three reasons for, and three reasons against, each idea below. Then discuss your views. As a group, form an opinion about each idea.

requiring employers to offer workers 12 weeks of parental leave
paying teachers less when their students fail
banning private cars from the downtown areas of big cities

A: What do you think about requiring employers to offer workers 12 weeks of parental leave?
B: I think it's a good idea. Parents should be allowed to stay with their babies . . .

offering a different opinion

That sounds interesting, but I think . . .
That's not a bad idea. On the other hand, I feel . . .
You may have a point. However, I think . . .

B **CLASS ACTIVITY** Share your group's opinions and reasons. Who has the most persuasive reasons for and against each position?

5 LISTENING Something has got to be done!

A Listen to people discuss annoying situations. Number the situations they describe in the correct order from 1 to 3. (There are three extra situations.)

- ☐ using the phone on speaker in public places
- ☐ using a cell phone on a plane
- ☐ posting selfies on social media
- ☐ taking selfies in crowded places
- ☐ not having signs about cell phones in public places
- ☐ texting in a movie theater

B Listen again. What solutions do they suggest for each situation?

1. ______________________________
2. ______________________________
3. ______________________________

C **GROUP WORK** Do you agree or disagree with the solutions? What do you think should be done about each problem?

6 INTERCHANGE 15 On the wrong side of the law

What if you could make the rules? Go to Interchange 15 on page 130.

7 WORD POWER Community issues

A **PAIR WORK** Which of these issues are problems in your community? Check (✓) the appropriate boxes.

- ☐ bullying
- ☐ homelessness
- ☐ inadequate health care
- ☐ irregular trash collection
- ☐ lack of affordable child care
- ☐ noise pollution
- ☐ overcrowded classrooms
- ☐ stray animals
- ☐ street crime
- ☐ vandalism

vandalism

B **GROUP WORK** Join another pair of students. Which three problems concern your group the most? What should or can be done about them?

8 CONVERSATION It's not easy, is it?

A Listen and practice.

Mara: I need to find a new apartment. I can't stand the noise from all those bars and clubs in my neighborhood anymore.

Ted: I can imagine. But it isn't easy to find a nice apartment in a quiet neighborhood, is it?

Mara: No, it's not! And my rent is already sky-high. I'm having a hard time making ends meet.

Ted: I know. Everything is really expensive nowadays, isn't it?

Mara: It sure is. You know, I'm looking for child care for my baby, but I just can't find anything affordable in the area.

Ted: The city should provide free child care to working families.

Mara: I think so, too. But unfortunately, the mayor doesn't.

B Listen to the rest of the conversation. What is Ted concerned about?

9 GRAMMAR FOCUS

Tag questions for opinions

Affirmative statement + negative tag	Negative statement + affirmative tag
Everything is really expensive nowadays, **isn't it**?	It isn't easy to find a nice apartment, **is it**?
There are lots of clubs around, **aren't there**?	There aren't any noise pollution laws, **are there**?
Mara likes her apartment, **doesn't she**?	Her neighbors don't make much noise, **do they**?
The city should provide child care, **shouldn't it**?	You can't sleep because of the noise, **can you**?

GRAMMAR PLUS see page 146

A Add tag questions to these statements. Then compare with a partner.

1. There aren't enough shelters for the homeless, . . . ?
2. Vandalism makes a neighborhood very unpleasant, . . . ?
3. In overcrowded classrooms, teachers can't give enough attention to students, . . . ?
4. School bullying is a major problem in most schools, . . . ?
5. There are more street crimes in big cities than in small towns, . . . ?
6. The government should provide adequate health care to everyone, . . . ?
7. The city doesn't do enough for stray animals, . . . ?
8. It isn't easy to save money these days, . . . ?

B What are some things you feel strongly about in your school or city? Write six statements with tag questions.

C **GROUP WORK** Take turns reading your statements. Other students respond by giving their opinions.

A: Public transportation isn't adequate, is it?
B: No, it isn't. There should be more bus lines.
C: On the other hand, the subway system is very efficient . . .

10 PRONUNCIATION Intonation in tag questions

A Listen and practice. Use falling intonation in tag questions when you are giving an opinion and expect the other person to agree.

Noise pollution is a serious problem in our city, isn't it?

Governments should offer child care to all working families, shouldn't they?

B **PAIR WORK** Take turns reading the statements with tag questions from Exercise 9, part A. Give your own opinions when responding.

11 LISTENING Let's face it.

A Listen to people give their opinions about issues in the news. What issues are they talking about?

	Issue	Opinions for	Opinions against
1.			
2.			

B Listen again. Write the different opinions that you hear.

C **GROUP WORK** What do you think about the issues in part A? Give your own opinions.

12 WRITING There ought to be a law.

A Think about a local problem that needs to be solved, and write a persuasive essay suggesting a new law to help solve it. Be creative! Use these questions to help you.

What is the problem, and how does it affect your community?
What can be done to help solve it?
Who might disagree with you, and how will you convince him or her that your law is a good idea?

> *The water crisis affects people all over the world. I think cities should be required to recycle their water. Also, people shouldn't be permitted to use clean drinking water to wash their cars and water their gardens. If people used recycled water, . . .*

B **GROUP WORK** Try to convince your classmates to pass your new law. Then vote on it.

13 READING

A Look at the title and the picture. What do you think plagiarism is?

HOME NEWS ARTICLES COMMUNITY

THAT'S PLAGIARISM?

POSTED AUGUST 21

If a teacher or your boss called you aside and said that he or she suspected you of plagiarism, how would you react? You'd probably be honestly confused. Nowadays, there are so many sources of information available that you can copy from with a single click. Many people don't even realize that they're committing plagiarism. Whether it's intentional or not, using someone else's information is stealing, and stealing is definitely a big deal.

The confusion about ownership comes from the fact that articles, photos, blogs, and social media posts are so easy to access – and just as easy to copy. When you see the same article on various websites, it's fairly natural to assume that it's public property. If a resource like Wikipedia offers material that can be critiqued and changed by its readers, that must be free for the taking, right? But that simply is not the case. Everything that has been written, drawn, photographed, or recorded, and released to the public, belongs to someone. Even your friends' comments on your social media page belong to them, not to you.

To avoid plagiarism, here are a few basic points to keep in mind. When writing a paper, if you get ideas or wording from someone else's writing, you must include the name of the writer or the source. If you find a few articles that you want to use, and you think taking a few points from each article and combining them makes the content yours, it's just not the case. This kind of "masked" plagiarism is very easy to spot, and it will get you into trouble. But really, just asking yourself a simple question should be enough: "Are all of these words my own?" If the answer is yes, you're in the clear.

In the end, the best approach is to write down the source for any material you quote from directly, and to assume that if it's public, it isn't yours. Plagiarism is a serious problem and can have serious consequences – even if it's totally accidental. Besides, putting ideas into your own words can make you a better writer, and a better thinker as well.

B Read the article. Then answer the questions.

1. What is the author's main purpose in writing the piece?
2. Why might it be easy to commit plagiarism by accident?
3. What question should you ask yourself in order to avoid plagiarism?

C Look at the following situations. Do you think they are describing plagiarism or not? If they are, do you think it was accidental or intentional?

1. Stacy copied a paragraph from a travel website and pasted it into her essay about Aruba. She put it into quotation marks and included the name and link for the website.
2. John works for a bank. He copied a paragraph from a website. He changed some words and rearranged some of the sentences. He did not indicate where it came from. He used it in a brochure for the bank.
3. Julie read an article online and later wrote her own essay about the same subject. Some of her wording was exactly the same as the online article.
4. Mitch borrowed a friend's essay to get some ideas for his own. Their teacher said that their essays were almost identical.

D **PAIR WORK** Sometimes famous musicians get in trouble for putting out songs that sound like someone else's. Do you think this is plagiarism? What, if anything, should be done about it?

16 Reaching your goals

- Discuss personal accomplishments
- Discuss goals

1 SNAPSHOT

Some Common Goals and Dreams

- ☐ win a competition
- ☐ make a lot of money
- ☐ get a promotion
- ☐ become famous
- ☐ learn to travel light
- ☐ find true love
- ☐ run a marathon
- ☐ learn to live with less
- ☐ be able to help others
- ☐ be respected
- ☐ have a healthy lifestyle
- ☐ plant a tree

Which of these goals do you think are the most difficult to achieve? Which are the easiest? Why?
Do you have the same goals? Check (✓) them.
What other goals or wishes do you have?

2 PERSPECTIVES Personal accomplishments

A Listen to people talk about their accomplishments. Match the statements and the people.

1. For me, my greatest accomplishment is the feeling that I've been able to help kids develop their potential and achieve their goals. ______
2. I worked hard in school, but I never managed to get good grades. However, I've just published my first book – and it's a best seller! ______
3. Last year, I ran my first marathon. I didn't win, but I was able to finish it, and I was very proud of myself. ______
4. No one believed in me in the beginning, but I've managed to make a living from my music for the past 5 years. ______
5. I felt I had reached one of my lifetime goals when I managed to quit my nine-to-five job to make a living traveling and sharing my experiences. ______

a. an amateur athlete
b. a teacher
c. a writer
d. a travel blogger
e. a musician

B **GROUP WORK** Do you share any similar accomplishments? Which ones?

3 GRAMMAR FOCUS

Talking about past accomplishments

With the simple past	With the present perfect
I **managed** to quit my nine-to-five job two years ago.	I**'ve managed** to make a living with my music.
I **didn't manage** to get good grades in school.	I **haven't managed** to record an album yet.
I **was able** to finish the marathon last year.	I**'ve been able** to help kids achieve their goals.
I **wasn't able** to travel much on my last job.	I **haven't been able** to achieve many of my goals.

GRAMMAR PLUS *see page 147*

A What are some of your latest accomplishments? Complete the statements with *have*, *haven't*, *was*, or *wasn't* to make them true for you.

1. I __________ managed to eat a healthy diet.
2. I __________ been able to help others.
3. I __________ met the person who's right for me.
4. I __________ made an important career move.
5. I __________ able to get a degree.
6. I __________ learned important life skills.

B **PAIR WORK** Compare your sentences in part A. What accomplishments do you have in common?

C **GROUP WORK** Complete the statements with your own information. Then share them with your classmates.

I have been able to ____________________.
I have managed to ____________________.
I haven't been able to ____________________.
I haven't managed to ____________________.

A: I've managed to take a trip abroad.
B: What countries did you visit?
A: I went to New Zealand three years ago.
C: Really? I've always wanted to go to New Zealand. How did you like it?

4 PRONUNCIATION Stress and rhythm

A Listen and practice. Notice how stressed words and syllables occur with a regular rhythm.

I managed to accomplish a lot while I was in college.

I haven't managed to get a promotion yet.

I was able to share my experiences with the world.

B **PAIR WORK** Take turns reading the sentences in the grammar box in Exercise 3. Pay attention to stress and rhythm.

5 LISTENING A different perspective

A Listen to two people answer two interview questions. Write the obstacles they faced and what they did about them in the chart.

	Mr. Sandberg	Ms. Rowe
Obstacle		
What he or she did		
What he or she learned		

B Listen again. What did each person learn from his or her experience? Complete the chart.

C **PAIR WORK** Discuss an obstacle that you managed to overcome. What did you learn?

6 WORD POWER Antonyms

A Complete the pairs of opposites with the words in the box. Then compare with a partner.

compassionate   cynical   dependent   rigid   timid   unimaginative

1. adaptable ≠ __________
2. courageous ≠ __________
3. insensitive ≠ __________
4. resourceful ≠ __________
5. self-sufficient ≠ __________
6. upbeat ≠ __________

B **GROUP WORK** How many words or things can you associate with each word in part A?

A: What words or things do you associate with *resourceful*?
B: Capable.
C: Good at solving problems.

7 DISCUSSION Inspirational sayings

A Read the quotes. Which one inspires you the most?

1. The greatest pleasure in life is doing what people say you can't do.
2. Discipline is the bridge between goals and achievements.
3. No matter what you have achieved, somebody helped you.
4. Fall down seven times, stand up eight.
5. Success isn't about how much money you make. It's about the difference you make in people's lives.

B **GROUP WORK** Discuss and justify your choices.

A: I like the first quote because, even though my friends weren't sure I could do it, I managed to graduate from high school early. That felt great!
B: You must have been resourceful! But someone helped you, too, didn't they?
C: That's why I like the third quote. No one achieves anything all on their own.

8 CONVERSATION Where do you see yourself?

A Listen and practice.

Interviewer: Tell me a bit more about yourself. What's your greatest accomplishment?

Mike: I think my most important accomplishment was the development of a mobile app during my internship last summer.

Interviewer: And did you manage to finish the project?

Mike: Yes, I was able to deliver the app before the end of my internship, and it has already received lots of positive reviews from customers.

Interviewer: That's interesting. And where do you see yourself in five years?

Mike: Well, I know your company already hires remote workers, and that's one of my goals for the future. So, five years from now, I hope I'll be working from my laptop in some tropical country . . . a true digital nomad.

Interviewer: I see. And what do you hope you'll have achieved by then?

Mike: I'd like to have developed many other successful apps. And I hope I'll have seen more of the world.

B **CLASS ACTIVITY** What do you think of Mike's answers? How would you have answered the interviewer's questions?

9 GRAMMAR FOCUS

Describing goals and possible future accomplishments

With the future perfect	With *would like to have* + past participle
What do you hope you**'ll have achieved**?	**What would you like to have** achieved?
I hope I**'ll have seen** more of the world.	**I'd like to have developed** many successful apps.

GRAMMAR PLUS *see page 147*

A What are some goals you would like to have accomplished in the future? Complete the sentences.

1. By this time next year, I hope I'll have . . .
2. Three years from now, I'd like to have . . .
3. In 10 years, I'd like to have . . .
4. By the time I'm 60, I hope I'll have . . .

Montreal, Canada

B **PAIR WORK** Compare your sentences. What goals do you have in common?

A: By this time next year, I hope I'll have finished my English course.

B: Me, too. And I'd like to have spent some time in an English-speaking country, like . . .

10 LISTENING My dream career

A Listen to three young people describe their plans for the future. What do they hope they will have achieved by the time they're 30?

	 1. Hugo	 2. Erin	 3. Danny
What they hope they'll have achieved			
Their reasons			

B Listen again. Why does each person have his or her specific dream? List one reason for each person.

C **PAIR WORK** Who do you think has the most realistic expectations? the least realistic? Why?

11 INTERCHANGE 16 A digital nomad

Are you ready to work remotely? Take a quiz and find out.
Go to Interchange 16 on page 131.

12 WRITING A personal statement for an application

A Imagine you are applying to a school or for a job that requires a personal statement. Use these questions to organize your ideas. Make notes and then write a draft.

1. What has your greatest accomplishment been? Has it changed you in any way? How?
2. What are some interesting or unusual facts about yourself that make you a good choice for the job or school?
3. What is something you hope to have achieved 10 years from now? When, why, and how will you reach this goal? Will achieving it change you? Why or why not?

I think my greatest accomplishment has been getting accepted at a top university in my country. I've always worked very hard in school, and I've had some truly amazing teachers who . . .

There are two things I'd like to have achieved 10 years from now. First, I hope I'll have made a good start on my career . . .

B **GROUP WORK** Share your statements and discuss each person's accomplishments and goals. Who has the most unusual accomplishment or goal? the most realistic? the most ambitious?

13 READING

A Scan the article. Where is Michael Edwards from? What sport did he participate in?

Soaring Like an Eagle

Being highly successful in any field is pretty rare. It takes a combination of natural talent, luck, determination, and plenty of outside support for someone to make it big in sports, entertainment, or business. But what if competing is all that matters to you, whether you are likely to succeed or not? This was the goal of Michael "Eddie the Eagle" Edwards, and that he reached that goal was an amazing achievement.

Born in the U.K. in 1963, Michael was an enthusiastic downhill skier whose dream was to compete for Britain in world-class competitions. He would have liked to represent his country in the 1984 Winter Olympics, but there was a large number of downhill competitors, and Edwards didn't qualify. Seeing his chance elsewhere, he switched to ski jumping. Ski jumping training didn't cost nearly as much, and there was no competition for a place on the British team.

But a number of hurdles could have meant the end of Edwards's dream. He weighed more than most competitors, which put him at a disadvantage. He had no financial support for his training. Poor eyesight meant that he had to wear glasses under his goggles – not a good thing when they steamed up at high altitudes. But he didn't let any of this discourage him. He saw himself as a true lover of the sport who simply wanted the chance to compete. Winning wasn't the point. Having the opportunity to try was all he cared about. And nothing could stop him from trying.

In the end, Edwards took 55th place in the 1987 World Championships. He then went on to the Calgary Olympics in 1988, where he finished last in both of his events. Many athletes would have been embarrassed by this result, but he is proud of his achievement to this day. His determination to persevere against all the odds made him a global hero, and in 2016, the inspiring film *Eddie the Eagle* was made about his life.

B Read the article. Answer the questions.

1. According to the writer, how often do people become highly successful?
2. What were two disadvantages that Michael Edwards overcame?
3. How did Edwards do at the Calgary Olympics in 1988?

C Choose the correct answers.

1. Michael Edwards chose ski jumping instead of downhill skiing because . . .
   - **a.** it took less skill.
   - **b.** the equipment was cheaper.
   - **c.** there were few British ski jumpers.
2. After the Calgary Olympics, Edwards . . .
   - **a.** felt he had reached his goal.
   - **b.** was embarrassed by his results.
   - **c.** was glad it was over.
3. Michael Edwards is outstanding because of . . .
   - **a.** his determination to win.
   - **b.** his ability to overcome physical disabilities.
   - **c.** his enthusiasm for the sport.

D **PAIR WORK** Would you compete in something if you knew you were likely to lose? Why or why not?

Units 15–16 Progress check

SELF-ASSESSMENT

How well can you do these things? Check (✓) the boxes.

I can . . .	Very well	OK	A little
Give recommendations and opinions about rules (Ex. 1)	☐	☐	☐
Understand and express opinions, and seek agreement (Ex. 2)	☐	☐	☐
Describe qualities necessary to achieve particular goals (Ex. 3)	☐	☐	☐
Ask about and describe personal achievements and goals (Ex. 4)	☐	☐	☐

1 DISCUSSION It's the rule.

A PAIR WORK What kinds of rules do you think should be made for these places? Talk with your partner and make three rules for each. (Have fun! Don't make your rules too serious.)

office　　public pool
a health club　　an apartment building

B GROUP WORK Join another pair. Share your ideas. Do they agree?

A: Office workers should all be required to wear the same outfit.
B: That sounds interesting. Why?
A: Well, for one thing, people wouldn't need to spend so much money on clothes.

2 LISTENING My city

A Listen to people give opinions about their city. Check (✓) the correct responses to agree with their statements.

1. ☐ Yes, it should.
   ☐ No, it shouldn't.
2. ☐ Yes, it is.
   ☐ No, it isn't.
3. ☐ Yes, they are.
   ☐ No, there aren't.
4. ☐ Yes, it does.
   ☐ Yes, they do.
5. ☐ Yes, we do.
   ☐ No, we don't.
6. ☐ No, there isn't.
   ☐ Yes, it is.

B PAIR WORK Come up with three more opinions about your city with a partner. Ask your classmates and see if they agree or disagree.

A: There aren't enough nightlife options for teenagers, are there?
B: No, there aren't!

3 DISCUSSION Do you have what it takes?

A GROUP WORK What qualities are needed if you want to accomplish these goals? Decide on two qualities for each goal.

Goals	Qualities		
start your own business	adaptable	dependent	self-sufficient
live abroad for a year	compassionate	insensitive	timid
make a low-budget movie	courageous	resourceful	unimaginative
hike across your country	cynical	rigid	upbeat

A: To start your own business, you need to be resourceful.
B: Yeah, and you should be courageous too.

B PAIR WORK Does your partner have what it takes to accomplish the goals in part A? Interview him or her and find out.

A: Do you think you're resourceful?
B: Yes, I think so. I'm usually good at solving problems.

4 ROLE PLAY Students' profiles

Student A: Student B is going to interview you for the school website. Think about your accomplishments and goals. Then answer the questions.

Student B: You are interviewing Student A for the school website. Add two questions to the notebook paper below. Then start the interview.

Change roles and try the role play again.

What have you managed to accomplish in school?
What would you like to have achieved by the time you graduate?

Are you happy with your home?
Do you hope you will move someday?
Where would you like to live?

Have you been able to accomplish a lot in your career?
Where do you hope you'll be in 5 years?

____

____

WHAT'S NEXT?

Look at your Self-assessment again. Do you need to review anything?

Interchange activities

INTERCHANGE 1 Personality quiz

A PAIR WORK What is your personality type? Take turns using the quiz to interview each other. Then tally your answers and find out which category best describes you.

What's your personality type?

1. When you fail a test, do you:

- **a.** get really upset and decide to try much harder next time?
- **b.** go over your answers and learn from your mistakes?
- **c.** not care much about it?

2. When you work on a big project, do you:
- **a.** try to finish it as quickly as possible?
- **b.** work at it over a long period of time?
- **c.** put it off as long as possible?

3. When you do an assignment, do you:
- **a.** try to do a first-class job so people will notice?
- **b.** do it as well as you can without worrying too much?
- **c.** do only what you must to get it done?

4. When faced with a difficult challenge, do you:
- **a.** look forward to facing it?
- **b.** worry about dealing with it?
- **c.** try to avoid it?

5. Do you think the best way to get the most out of a day is to:
- **a.** do as many things as possible?
- **b.** take your time to get things done?
- **c.** do only those things you really have to?

6. When something doesn't work out the way you want it to, do you:
- **a.** get angry with yourself and others?
- **b.** think calmly about what to do next?
- **c.** give up, because it wasn't important anyway?

7. When people take a long time to finish something, do you:
- **a.** get impatient and do it yourself?
- **b.** gently ask them to do it more quickly?
- **c.** let them take their time?

8. When you are learning a new skill, do you:
- **a.** work very hard to master it quickly?
- **b.** do your best and often ask for help?
- **c.** take your time and enjoy the learning experience?

9. If you compare your goals with your friends' goals, do you:

- **a.** want to accomplish greater things than they do?
- **b.** hope to achieve similar things in life?
- **c.** not care if they set higher goals for themselves than you do?

10. When people are late for appointments, do you:
- **a.** get angry and stressed out?
- **b.** remember that you are sometimes late, too?
- **c.** not worry, because you are usually late, too?

11. When people are talking to you, do you:
- **a.** not listen and think about other things?
- **b.** listen and participate in the conversation?
- **c.** let them talk and agree with everything they say?

Scoring

Count how many a, b, and c answers your partner has. If there are . . .

mostly a answers: This person is a high achiever but can get very stressed.

mostly b answers: This person is the cool and steady type.

mostly c answers: This person is the easygoing or carefree type.

B GROUP WORK Compare your scores. Then suggest four characteristics of each personality type.

"A high achiever is the kind of person who . . . . He or she can't stand it when . . ."

INTERCHANGE 2 Networking

A PAIR WORK Imagine you and your partner are organizing a dinner party for new entrepreneurs and potential investors.

Read about each person on the guest list.

Home About News Business Community Sign in

ENTREPRENEURS

Gaston Lafont is 25, single, and a promising chef. He's friendly and ambitious, but he can be very moody. He's coming to the party to get celebrities and powerful business executives to invest in his restaurant.

Melissa Dominguez is 28, single, and a computer wizard. She puts her career ahead of her personal life and has few interests apart from her work. She needs funding for a new start-up company.

Don Hart is 32, married, and an environmentalist. He's egotistical, outspoken, and tends to start arguments. He wants to run for mayor and needs funding for his campaign.

Emma Stewart is 30, single, and a medical researcher. She's shy and introverted and has devoted her life to helping children around the world. She's currently developing a new vaccine for a widespread tropical disease.

INVESTORS

Mike Hunter is 54, a widower, and an oil tycoon. This millionaire is bossy and straightforward. His companies have been accused of destroying the environment in many countries.

Paola Di Matteo is 23, single, and a world-famous movie star. She's very private about her personal life, and she is interested in investing in young talent.

Joanne Parson is 42, single, and an art and nature lover. Wealthy and sociable, she takes part in several volunteer projects and gives substantial amounts of money to various causes around the world.

Ren Okawa is 38, married, and a stockbroker. He likes to invest in new companies and has helped many startups and young entrepreneurs succeed. He's smart, ambitious, and has sophisticated taste in art and food.

B PAIR WORK Discuss the possible seating arrangements for the party. Then complete this seating plan.

A: Let's seat Gaston next to Ren. Gaston is interested in finding investors for his new restaurant.

B: It might be better to put Ren next to Melissa. Ren likes to invest in start-ups, so . . .

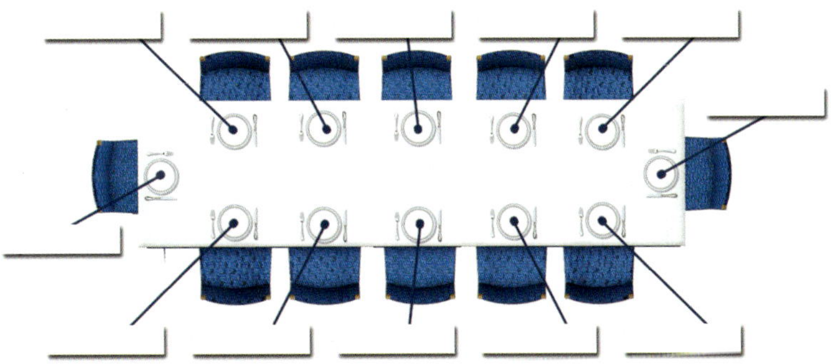

INTERCHANGE 3 Beg and borrow

A Imagine you own these items. Which ones would you be willing to lend to a friend? Which ones wouldn't you lend? Check (✓) a response for each item.

TENT

☐ wouldn't mind lending
☐ wouldn't want to lend

TABLET

☐ wouldn't mind lending
☐ wouldn't want to lend

CAR

☐ wouldn't mind lending
☐ wouldn't want to lend

MOUNTAIN BIKE

☐ wouldn't mind lending
☐ wouldn't want to lend

POWER DRILL

☐ wouldn't mind lending
☐ wouldn't want to lend

CLASS NOTES

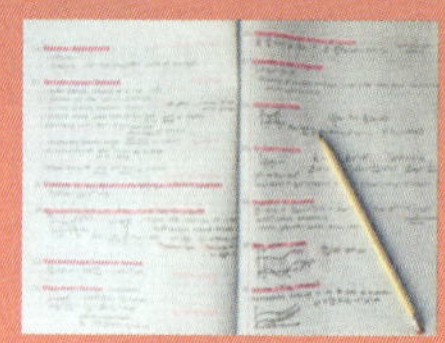

☐ wouldn't mind lending
☐ wouldn't want to lend

CAMERA

☐ wouldn't mind lending
☐ wouldn't want to lend

SLEEPING BAG

☐ wouldn't mind lending
☐ wouldn't want to lend

HEADPHONES

☐ wouldn't mind lending
☐ wouldn't want to lend

B **CLASS ACTIVITY** Go around the class and take turns asking to borrow each item in part A. Explain why you want to borrow it. When responding, say if you are willing to lend the item or not. If you won't lend something, say why.

A: Would you mind lending me your tent for the weekend? I want to go camping, but I got a hole in my tent.

B: I'm sorry, but I don't think I can. I might want to go camping this weekend, too!

OR

B: Sure. Just come over tonight and pick it up.

C **CLASS ACTIVITY** Who was able to borrow the most items?

INTERCHANGE 4 Spin a yarn

A **GROUP WORK** Place a pen on the CHARACTER spinner and spin it. Repeat for the other two spinners. Use the elements the pen points at to create a story. If the pen points at YOU DECIDE, you can use any element from that spinner, or you can invent a new one.

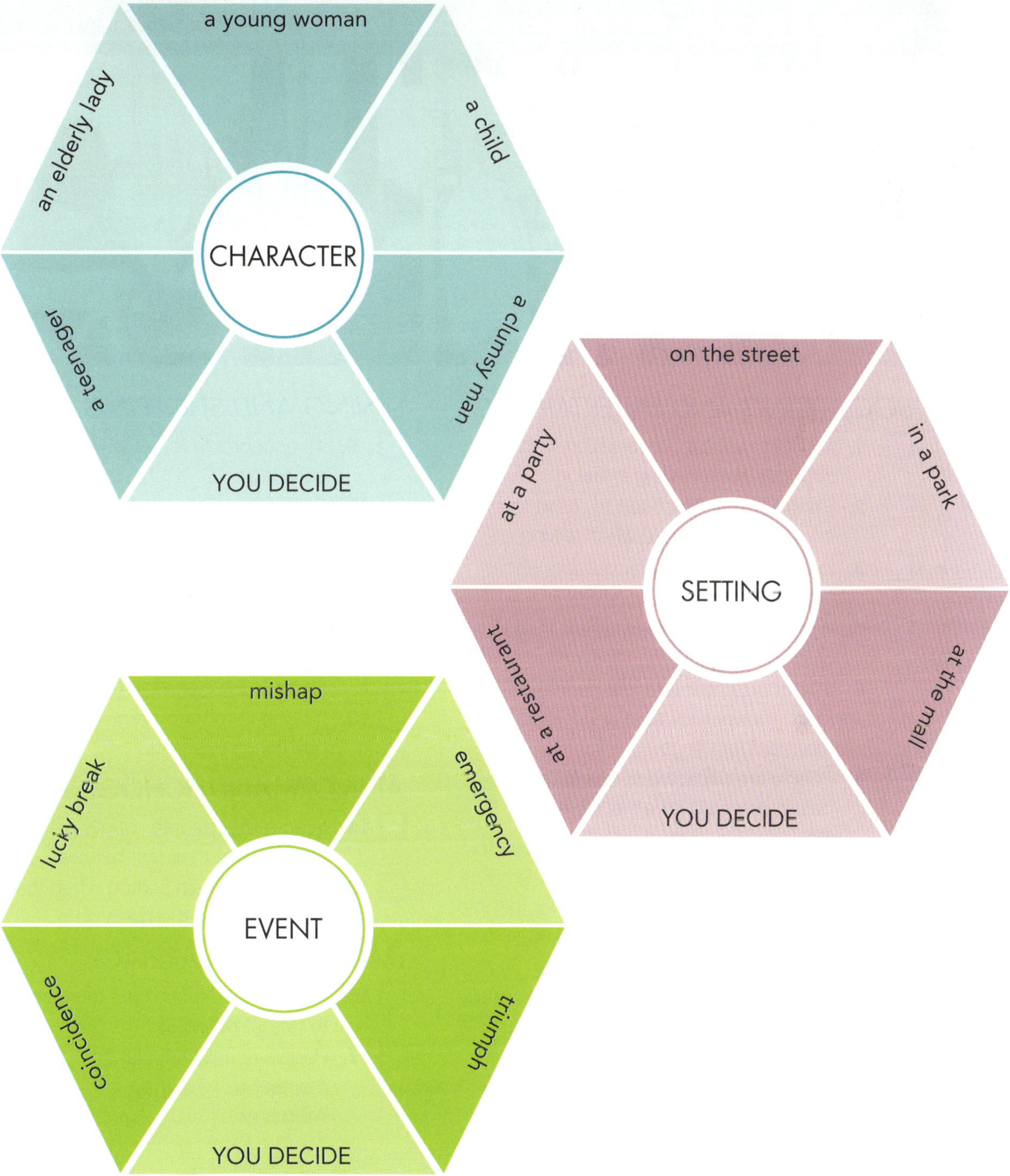

"One day a clumsy man was having dinner at a restaurant when . . ."

B **CLASS ACTIVITY** Share your group's stories with your classmates. Who created the most interesting story? the most unexpected? the most creative?

INTERCHANGE 5 Cultural dos and taboos

A These statements are generally true about cultural behavior in the United States. Check (✓) those that are true in your country.

COMPARING CULTURES

Find out how typical U.S. cultural behavior compares to yours!

SOCIALIZING AND ENTERTAINING

☐ **1.** It's OK to start a conversation with a stranger when waiting in line.

☐ **2.** People aren't supposed to stand too close to other people when talking.

☐ **3.** In general, people wear outdoor shoes inside their homes.

☐ **4.** Women often hug their female friends when they meet.

☐ **5.** It's not acceptable to ask people how much money they earn or how much they paid for things.

☐ **6.** People are expected to call or text before dropping by a friend's house.

☐ **7.** When invited to someone's home for dinner, people usually arrive on time.

☐ **8.** Gifts are normally opened when received.

DINING AND SHOPPING

☐ **9.** It's acceptable to eat while walking outside.

☐ **10.** Eating is not allowed while shopping in most stores.

☐ **11.** When eating in a restaurant, friends either split the cost of the meal or take turns paying.

☐ **12.** It's the custom to leave a 15–20% tip for the server at a restaurant.

☐ **13.** It's uncommon to bargain when you buy things in stores.

AT WORK AND SCHOOL

☐ **14.** In an office, people usually prefer to be called by their first names.

☐ **15.** Students remain seated when the teacher enters the classroom.

DATING AND MARRIAGE

☐ **16.** It's acceptable for most teenagers to go out on dates.

☐ **17.** People usually decide for themselves who they will marry.

B PAIR WORK Compare your answers with a partner. For the statements you didn't check, why do you think these behaviors are different in your country?

INTERCHANGE 6A Home makeover

Student A

A Look at this apartment. What's wrong with it? First, make a list of as many problems as you can find in each room.

B **PAIR WORK** Compare your lists. What are the similarities and differences in the problems between your picture and your partner's picture? Ask questions to find the differences.

A: What's wrong in the bedroom?

B: Well, in my picture, the walls need painting. And the curtains . . .

A: Oh, really? In my picture, the walls need to be painted, but the curtains . . . , and the window . . .

Student B

A Look at this apartment. What's wrong with it? First, make a list of as many problems as you can find in each room.

B **PAIR WORK** Compare your lists. What are the similarities and differences in the problems between your picture and your partner's picture? Ask questions to find the differences.

A: What's wrong in the bedroom?

B: Well, in my picture, the walls need painting. And the curtains . . .

A: Oh, really? In my picture, the walls need to be painted, but the curtains . . . , and the window . . .

INTERCHANGE 7 Take action!

A Read about these issues. Which one would you most likely protest?

A baby food company has been using genetically modified fruit and vegetables in their recipes to lower costs.

Congress is discussing a law that allows the government to shut down any website it considers inappropriate.

The city is going to close a public park to build a new bus terminal.

B **GROUP WORK** Find other students who chose the same issue. Then look at methods of protest. Which are the most effective for the issue you chose? Complete the chart.

METHOD OF PROTEST	VERY EFFECTIVE	SOMEWHAT EFFECTIVE	NOT EFFECTIVE
start an online campaign	☐	☐	☐
stage a sit-in	☐	☐	☐
organize a demonstration	☐	☐	☐
boycott a product or service	☐	☐	☐
ask people to sign an online petition	☐	☐	☐
contact local news stations	☐	☐	☐
contact your local government representative	☐	☐	☐
distribute pamphlets about the issue	☐	☐	☐
hold an awareness campaign in the community	☐	☐	☐
create posters and signs to hang up around town	☐	☐	☐

Develop a strategy to make your voices heard using the above methods or your own ideas.

C **CLASS ACTIVITY** How did you decide to deal with the issue? Present your group's strategy to the class.

INTERCHANGE 8 Making choices

A Complete this chart with information about yourself. Add one idea of your own.

two artistic skills I'd like to develop		
two adventurous activities I'd like to try		
two dances I'd like to learn		
two topics I'd like to learn more about		
two foreign languages I'd like to speak		
two dishes I'd like to learn how to cook		
two volunteer activities I'd like to do		
two courses I'd like to take		
two sports I'd like to play		
two skills I'd like to improve		
two ______________		

B **CLASS ACTIVITY** Ask three classmates to help you choose between the things you wrote down in part A. Write their recommendations in the chart.

Names:			
artistic skill			
adventurous activity			
dance			
topic			
foreign language			
dish			
volunteer activity			
course			
sport			
skill			
______________			

A: I don't know if I'd rather be a graffiti artist or a painter. What do you think?
B: Hmm. If I were you, I'd choose graffiti.
A: Why graffiti and not painting?
B: Well, that kind of street art is very popular nowadays. You could become famous, and . . .

C **GROUP WORK** What are your final choices? Who gave the best advice? Why?

INTERCHANGE 9 Absolutely not!

A PAIR WORK Read these comments made by parents. Why do you think they feel this way? Think of two arguments to support each point of view.

A: Why do you think they won't let their son go camping with his friends?
B: They probably think he's too young to take care of himself.
A: They may also feel that he . . .

B PAIR WORK Discuss the parents' decisions. Think of arguments for and against their points of view.

A: I think the parents should let their son go camping with his friends.
B: Why?
A: Because his friends are going, and he needs to learn to take care of himself.
B: I don't agree. I think he's too young. Teens shouldn't travel without an adult.

C CLASS ACTIVITY Take a vote. Do you agree with the parents? Why?

INTERCHANGE 10A History buff

Student A

A PAIR WORK Ask your partner these questions. Put a check (✓) if your partner gives the correct answer. (The correct answers are in **bold**.)

Frida Kahlo

Volkswagen Beetle

Alexander Fleming

TEST YOUR KNOWLEDGE

☐ 1. What nationality was the painter Frida Kahlo? Was she Spanish, **Mexican**, or Argentinian?

☐ 2. What was the first capital of the United States? Was it **Philadelphia**, New York, or Boston?

☐ 3. Who played 007 in the first James Bond movie? Was it Roger Moore, **Sean Connery**, or Pierce Brosnan?

☐ 4. When was the first Volkswagen Beetle car built? Was it during the 1920s, **1930s**, or 1940s?

☐ 5. Was Nelson Mandela a political activist from India, Angola, or **South Africa**?

☐ 6. When did the British return Hong Kong to China? Was it in 1987, **1997**, or 2007?

☐ 7. Who discovered penicillin? Was it **Alexander Fleming**, Charles Darwin, or Albert Einstein?

☐ 8. Which planet is closest to the sun? Is it Mars, **Mercury**, or Venus?

☐ 9. What Italian astronomer invented the thermometer in 1593? Was it Copernicus, Isaac Newton, or **Galileo**?

☐ 10. When did the first MP3 player hit the market in the US? Was it in 1978, 1988, or **1998**?

B PAIR WORK Answer the questions your partner asks you. Then compare quizzes. Who has the most correct answers?

C CLASS ACTIVITY Think of three more questions of your own. Can the rest of the class answer them?

INTERCHANGE 11 Good choices, bad choices

A PAIR WORK Play the board game. Follow these instructions.

1. Use small pieces of paper with your initials on them as markers.
2. Take turns tossing a coin:

Move one space.

Heads

Move two spaces.

Tails

3. When you land on a space, tell your partner what is true. Then say how things would have been different. For example:
   "When I was younger, I didn't pay attention in class. If I had paid attention in class, I would have gotten better grades."
   OR
   "When I was younger, I paid attention in class. If I hadn't paid attention in class, I wouldn't have won a scholarship."

B CLASS ACTIVITY Who was responsible when they were younger? Who was rebellious? Tell the class.

INTERCHANGE 10B History buff

Student B

A **PAIR WORK** Answer the questions your partner asks you.

B **PAIR WORK** Ask your partner these questions. Put a check (✓) if your partner gives the correct answer. (The correct answers are in **bold**.) Then compare quizzes. Who has the most correct answers?

Mona Lisa

a compass

Berlin Wall

TEST YOUR KNOWLEDGE

☐ 1. What was the former name of New York City? Was it New England, New London, or **New Amsterdam**?

☐ 2. What artist painted the *Mona Lisa*? Was it **Leonardo da Vinci**, Michelangelo, or Raphael?

☐ 3. When did Walt Disney make his first cartoon movie? Was it in 1920, **1937**, or 1947?

☐ 4. Who used the first magnetic compass? Was it **the Chinese**, the Portuguese, or the Dutch?

☐ 5. Constantinople was an earlier name of what city? Was it Cairo, Mumbai, or **Istanbul**?

☐ 6. When did the Berlin Wall come down? Was it in 1979, **1989**, or 1999?

☐ 7. Where was Marie Curie, the first woman to receive a Nobel Prize, born? Was it in **Poland**, France, or England?

☐ 8. Who was the first human in space? Was it **Yuri Gagarin**, Neil Armstrong, or John Glenn?

☐ 9. What did Thomas Edison invent in 1879? Was it the television, the telephone, or the **lightbulb**?

☐ 10. In which year did Mexico gain its independence? Was it in 1721, **1821**, or 1921?

C **CLASS ACTIVITY** Think of three more questions of your own. Can the rest of the class answer them?

INTERCHANGE 12 Advertising taglines

A **PAIR WORK** Read these popular slogans for products. Match the slogans with the product types.

1. Think different. ______	**a.** a soft drink
2. Unforgettable happens here. ______	**b.** a technology company
3. Taste the feeling. ______	**c.** an amusement park
4. All the news that's fit to print. ______	**d.** sports clothing
5. Impossible is nothing. ______	**e.** potato chips
6. Bet you can't eat just one. ______	**f.** a daily newspaper
7. Stay with us, and feel like home. ______	**g.** fast food
8. Reach out and touch someone. ______	**h.** automobiles
9. I'm loving it. ______	**i.** a game console
10. Live in your world. Play in ours. ______	**j.** a hotel
11. Melts in your mouth, not in your hands. ______	**k.** a telephone service
12. Built for the road ahead. ______	**l.** chocolate candy

B **PAIR WORK** Join another pair and compare your answers. Then check your answers at the bottom of the page.

C **GROUP WORK** Think of a product. Then create your own slogan for it and add a logo. Consider a design and colors that are suitable for the product.

A: Any ideas for a product?
B: What about an online store for used toys?
C: Sounds interesting. Let's try to think of some catchy slogans.
D: How about, "Play again!"? Or maybe . . .

D **CLASS ACTIVITY** Present your slogans to the class. Who has the catchiest ones?

1. b; **2.** c; **3.** a; **4.** f; **5.** d; **6.** e; **7.** j; **8.** k; **9.** g; **10.** i; **11.** l; **12.** h

INTERCHANGE 13 Think of the possibilities!

A PAIR WORK What do you think might have happened in each situation? Talk about possibilities for each situation.

1

Pete made a fortune in the stock market. He's now working at a burger joint.

2

Lisa went grocery shopping yesterday afternoon. She hasn't come back home yet.

3

Jim was the best salesperson in the company for the past 10 years. He just got fired.

4

Clara had everything ready for her dream vacation in Tahiti. She's on the bus heading to her parents' home.

A: Maybe Pete made some bad investments.

B: Or he might have spent all his money on . . .

useful expressions	
Maybe he/she was . . . when . . .	He/She may have . . . when . . .
Or perhaps he/she was . . .	He/She might have . . .

B GROUP WORK Agree on one explanation for each situation and share it with the class. Be ready to answer any questions.

INTERCHANGE 14 Celebrities

A Prepare to play a guessing game.

- Write the names of five celebrities on slips of paper. Names can include people in history, movie stars, singers, politicians, writers, etc.
- Mix all the slips in a bag.

B **GROUP WORK** Each player takes turns picking a slip for his or her group to guess.

A: She's a celebrity who was born in London.
B: Is she a movie star?
A: No, she's a singer and songwriter who has a beautiful voice.
C: I think I know the answer. It's . . .

C **CLASS ACTIVITY** Which celebrities were easier to guess? Which were the most difficult? Who gave the best clues?

Nico Rosberg

Sofia Vergara

Albert Einstein

Sally Ride

INTERCHANGE 15 On the wrong side of the law

A PAIR WORK What punishment (if any) is appropriate for each possible offense? Why? Complete the chart.

OFFENSE	PUNISHMENT
1 parking in a disabled parking space without a permit	
2 posting offensive comments online	
3 leaving trash on public streets	
4 riding the subway without paying the fare	
5 failing to clean up after a dog	
6 pickpocketing	
7 scratching paint off another person's car	
8 crossing the street in dangerous places	
9 driving without a seat belt	
10 riding a motorcycle without a helmet	
11 hacking into a government computer	
12 ____________ (your own idea)	

A: What do you think should be done about people who park in a disabled parking space without a permit?
B: They should be required to pay a heavy fine because it may cause problems for people with disabilities.
A: I don't agree. I think . . .

possible punishments

- receive a warning
- spend some time in jail
- pay a fine
- lose a driver's license
- get suspended
- do community service
- be banned from using the Internet

B GROUP WORK Join another pair of students. Then compare and discuss your lists. Do you agree or disagree? Try to convince each other that you are right!

INTERCHANGE 16 A digital nomad

A PAIR WORK Interview your partner. Would he or she be a happy digital nomad?

Is the digital nomad lifestyle **right for you?**

Do you dream of working from a beach paradise? Are you ready to hit the road and make a living while traveling the world? Take our quiz and find out.

1. Have you traveled much before?
- ☐ **a.** I've traveled with my family in our country.
- ☐ **b.** Not yet, but I hope to have seen more of the world by the time I retire.
- ☐ **c.** I've been to a couple of continents and seen some amazing things!

2. Are you resourceful?
- ☐ **a.** Well, I can always count on my friends to help me when I need it.
- ☐ **b.** Yes, and I can always find the answers I need on the Internet.
- ☐ **c.** Yes, I'm good at finding opportunities everywhere.

3. When you pack for a long weekend, what do you take with you?
- ☐ **a.** A big suitcase with everything I might need – you never know what might happen.
- ☐ **b.** A small bag with the essentials.
- ☐ **c.** A toothbrush and a change of clothes. I like to travel light.

4. Are you flexible and adaptable?
- ☐ **a.** I try to be, but I don't always succeed.
- ☐ **b.** Yes, if you give me some time to adjust.
- ☐ **c.** Definitely. I've managed to survive under the most challenging circumstances.

5. Have you ever traveled all by yourself?
- ☐ **a.** Of course not. I need family and friends around at all times.
- ☐ **b.** No, but I think I'd enjoy it.
- ☐ **c.** Sure. I often take vacations alone. It's a great opportunity to meet new people.

6. Are you ready to give up a fixed salary?
- ☐ **a.** No. I need to have a steady income. It's important for me to know how much money I'll be making for the next 12 months.
- ☐ **b.** Well, I can live on very little money – I've done it before.
- ☐ **c.** I'm good at managing my money, and I always have some savings, so that wouldn't be a problem.

7. Are you self-motivated, or do you depend on others to get you going?
- ☐ **a.** I need to know that my boss or my teachers are around and that I can count on them.
- ☐ **b.** It depends. If I'm really involved with a project, I'm more independent; if not . . .
- ☐ **c.** Definitely. I know what I have to do, and I always finish the work on time.

8. How do you feel about changes?
- ☐ **a.** I like to have a set routine. Changes make me feel uncomfortable.
- ☐ **b.** They can be a challenge, but they also help me grow.
- ☐ **c.** Changes are always welcome. New things inspire and motivate me.

Score the quiz by counting the number of a's, b's, and c's.
Mostly a's: The digital nomad lifestyle is not for you.
Mostly b's: You'd probably be happy being a digital nomad, but you might miss your current life.
Mostly c's: What are you doing here? Go grab your things and hit the road!

B CLASS ACTIVITY Compare your findings. Who is ready to become a digital nomad?

Grammar plus

UNIT 1

1 Relative pronouns page 3

- A relative pronoun – *who* or *that* – is necessary when the pronoun is the subject of the clause: I'd love to meet someone **who/that** is considerate. (NOT: I'd love to meet ~~someone is considerate~~.)
- When the pronoun is the object of the clause, *who* and *that* can be left out: I'd like a roommate **who/that** I have a lot in common with. OR I'd like a roommate I have a lot in common with.

Complete the conversation with *who* or *that*. Put an ✗ when a relative pronoun isn't necessary.

A: Ana, have you met Clint – the guy __✗__ Laurie is going to marry?
B: Oh, Clint and I have been friends for years. In fact, I'm the one _____ introduced Laurie and Clint.
A: Do you think they're right for each other?
B: Definitely. They're two people _____ have a lot in common – but not *too* much.
A: What does that mean?
B: Well, you don't want a partner _____ doesn't have his or her own interests. Couples _____ do everything together usually don't last very long.
A: I guess you're right, but the opposite isn't good, either. My last girlfriend was someone _____ I had nothing in common with. She wasn't the kind of girl _____ I could talk to easily.
B: Well, you can talk to *me* easily. . . .

2 *It* clauses + adverbial clauses with *when* page 6

- In sentences with an *it* clause + an adverbial clause with *when*, the word *it* refers to and means the same as the adverbial clause with *when*. The *it* in these sentences is necessary and cannot be left out: I hate **it when** people talk on a cell phone in an elevator. (NOT: ~~I hate when~~ people . . .) **It** bothers me **when** people talk on a cell phone in an elevator. (NOT: ~~Bothers~~ me when people . . .)

Rewrite the sentences using the words in parentheses.

1. I can't stand it when people call me before 8:00 A.M. (it really bothers me)
   It really bothers me when people call me before 8:00 a.m.
2. It upsets me when I don't have enough time to study for an exam. (I hate it)
   ____
3. I don't mind it when friends talk to me about their problems. (it doesn't bother me)
   ____
4. I don't like it when I forget a co-worker's name. (it embarrasses me)
   ____
5. It makes me happy when my friends send me videos. (I love it)
   ____
6. I hate it when I have to wait for someone. (it upsets me)
   ____

UNIT 2

1 Gerund phrases page 9

- A gerund phrase as a subject takes a singular verb: Taking care of children **is** a rewarding job. (NOT: Taking care of children ~~are~~ a rewarding job.)
- There are some common verb + preposition expressions (for example, *dream about, feel like, talk about, think about*) and adjective + preposition phrases (for example, *good/bad at, excited by/about, interested in, tired of, used to*) that are followed by a gerund: I'm **thinking about looking for** a new job. I'm **tired of working** long hours.

Complete the sentences with the correct gerund forms of the verbs in the box.

✓ become	have	make	stand	travel
change	learn	solve	take	work

1. My brother's very interested in ___becoming___ a flight attendant. He dreams about ______________ to new places.
2. I'm excited about ______________ a Japanese class next semester. I enjoy ______________ languages.
3. You wouldn't like ______________ in a restaurant. You'd get tired of ______________ on your feet throughout the long shifts!
4. Our teacher is very good at ______________ problems. Maybe she should think about ______________ careers to become a guidance counselor.
5. ______________ a living as a photographer could be challenging. ______________ an impressive portfolio is really important to attract new clients and employers.

2 Comparisons page 11

- When making general comparisons with count nouns, use *a/an* + singular noun or no article + plural noun: **A pilot** earns more than **a flight attendant**. **Pilots** earn more than **flight attendants**. (NOT: ~~The~~ pilots earn more than ~~the~~ flight attendants.)

Make comparisons with the information below. Add articles and other words when necessary.

1. architect / more education / hairstylist
   An architect needs more education than a hairstylist.
2. college professor / earn more / elementary school teacher
   ____
3. nurses / worse hours / psychiatrists
   ____
4. working as a police officer / as dangerous / being a firefighter
   ____
5. taxi driver / not as well paid / electrician
   ____
6. being a tour guide / less interesting / being an actor
   ____

UNIT 3

1 Requests with modals, *if* clauses, and gerunds page 17

- Use the simple past form – not the gerund or simple present form – after *if* with *Would you mind . . . ?* and *Would it be all right . . . ?*: **Would you mind if I used** your car? **Would it be all right if I used** your car? (NOT: Would you mind if I ~~using~~ your car? OR Would it be all right if I ~~use~~ your car?)

Read the situations. Then complete the requests.

1. You want to borrow a friend's underwater camera for a diving trip.
   A: I was wondering if *I could borrow your underwater camera.*
   B: Sure. That's fine. Just please be careful with it.
2. You want to use your roommate's computer.
   A: Is it OK ______
   B: You can use it, but please don't drink near it.
3. Your neighbor has a car. You need a ride to class.
   A: Would you mind ______
   B: I'd be glad to. What time should I pick you up?
4. You want your brother to help you move on Saturday.
   A: Can you ______
   B: I'm sorry. I'm busy all weekend.
5. You would like a second piece of your aunt's cherry pie.
   A: Would it be all right ______
   B: Yes, of course! Just pass me your plate.
6. You want to borrow your cousin's red sweater.
   A: Could you ______
   B: Sorry. I don't like it when other people wear my clothes.

2 Indirect requests page 20

- In indirect requests with negative infinitives, *not* comes before – not between – the infinitive: Could you tell Allie **not to be** late? (NOT: Could you tell Allie ~~to not be~~ late?)

Complete the indirect requests. Ask someone to deliver the messages to Susie.

1. Are you busy this weekend? → Could *you ask Susie if she's busy this weekend?*
2. Do you want to hang out with me? → Can ______
3. Text me. → Can ______
4. Do you know my address? → Can ______
5. Don't forget to write. → Could ______
6. What are you doing Saturday? → Can ______
7. Do you have plans on Sunday? → Could ______

UNIT 4

1 Past continuous vs. simple past page 23

- Verbs for non-actions or states are rarely used in the past continuous: I **wanted** to stop, but I couldn't. (NOT: I ~~was wanting~~ to stop . . .)

Circle the best forms to complete the conversations.

1. **A:** How **did you break** / **were you breaking** your arm?
   B: It's a crazy story! Ramon and I **rode** / **were riding** our bikes in the park when a cat **ran** / **was running** out in front of me. I **went** / **was going** pretty fast, so when I **tried** / **was trying** to stop, I **went** / **was going** off the road and **fell** / **was falling**.
   A: That's terrible! **Did you go** / **Were you going to** the hospital after it **happened** / **was happening**?
   B: Yes. Luckily, we **weren't** / **weren't being** too far from City Hospital, so we **went** / **were going** there.
2. **A:** You'll never guess what **happened** / **was happening** to me this morning!
   B: What?
   A: Well, I **brushed** / **was brushing** my teeth when suddenly the water **went** / **was going** off. I **had** / **was having** toothpaste all over my mouth, and I couldn't wash it off.
   B: So what **did you do** / **were you doing**?
   A: Fortunately, I **had** / **was having** a big bottle of water in the refrigerator, so I **used** / **was using** that water to rinse my mouth.

2 Past perfect page 25

- Use the past perfect to show that one past action happened before another past action:
  I **wasn't able to** pay for lunch because I **had left** my wallet at work.
  PAST ———— X ———————— X ———— NOW
  had left my wallet — wasn't able to pay

Combine the two ideas into one with a past event and a past perfect event. Use *when* or *because*.

1. The museum closed. A thief stole a famous painting earlier.
   The museum closed because a thief had stolen a famous painting earlier.
2. We finished cleaning the house. Then our guests arrived.
   ____
3. Someone robbed my house yesterday. I left the window open.
   ____
4. There was no food in the house. We forgot to stop at the supermarket.
   ____
5. I called her three times. She finally answered.
   ____
6. I knew about the problem. Your brother told me about it.
   ____

UNIT 5

1 Noun phrases containing relative clauses page 31

- The relative pronoun *who* or *that* can be left out in noun phrases as subjects and as objects. These four sentences have exactly the same meaning: One thing I'd be nervous about is getting lost. One thing that I'd be nervous about is getting lost. Getting lost is one thing I'd be nervous about. Getting lost is one thing that I'd be nervous about.

Answer the questions using the words in parentheses. Write each sentence two ways. Leave out the relative pronouns.

If you went to live in a foreign country, . . .

1. Who would you miss a lot? (person: my best friend)
   a. *One person I'd miss a lot is my best friend.*
   b. *My best friend is one person I'd miss a lot.*
2. What would you be very interested in? (things: the food and the music)
   a. ______
   b. ______
3. What would you be worried about? (something: not understanding the customs)
   a. ______
   b. ______
4. Who would you stay in touch with? (people: my brother and sister)
   a. ______
   b. ______
5. What would you feel insecure about? (thing: speaking a new language)
   a. ______
   b. ______

2 Expectations page 33

- Use the base form of a verb – not the gerund – after these expressions for expectations: *be the custom to, be supposed to, be expected to, be acceptable to*: It's the custom to **arrive** a little late. (NOT: It's the custom to ~~arriving~~ a little late.)

Complete the sentences with the clauses in the box.

it's not acceptable to show up without calling first.
it's the custom for them to sit across from each other.
you're expected to reply within a few days.
you're supposed to bring a gift.
✓ you're supposed to shake his or her hand.

1. When you meet someone for the first time, *you're supposed to shake his or her hand.*
2. When a friend sends you an email, ______
3. If you want to visit someone, ______
4. If you invite a married couple to dinner, ______
5. When you go to a birthday party, ______

UNIT 6

1 Describing problems 1 page 37

■ The simple past and the past participle of regular verbs are the same: I **chipped** the vase. The vase is **chipped**. BUT Many irregular verbs have different simple past and past participle forms: I **tore** my jacket. My jacket is **torn**.

Complete the conversations with the correct words from the box.

are stained	**has a dent**	**✓ have a tear**	**is broken**	**is scratched**
has a chip	**has a stain**	**is a hole**	**is leaking**	**some damage**

1. **A:** Oh, no! These jeans ___have a tear___ in them.
   B: And they ____________, too.
2. **A:** This table has ____________ on top.
   B: I know. The wood ____________ because my son drags his toy cars on it.
3. **A:** Why are you drinking out of that glass? It ____________ in it.
   B: Oh, I didn't see it. That's why it ____________.
4. **A:** Someone hit my car today. Look! The door ____________ in it.
   B: I see that. Your back light ____________, too.
5. **A:** I bought this blouse yesterday, but I have to take it back. There ____________ in it.
   B: It's really cute, but that's not the only problem. It ____________ on it, too.

2 Describing problems 2 page 39

■ Use the past participle – not the present participle or gerund – with passive forms: The oven needs to be **fixed**. (NOT: The oven needs to be ~~fixing~~.)

A Complete the conversation with the verbs in parentheses. Use *need* + passive infinitive in A's lines and *need* + gerund in B's lines.

A: Look at this place! A lot of work ___needs to be done___ (do) before we move in.
B: You're not kidding. Let's make a list. First, the walls ___need painting___ (paint).
A: Right. And the windows ____________ (wash). Add the rug to your list: It really ____________ (clean). Do you think it ____________ (dry-clean)?
B: No, I think we can do it ourselves. It ____________ (shampoo). We can rent a machine for that.
A: And what about the ceiling fan? I think it ____________ (replace). Fans aren't too expensive.
B: OK. I've added it to the list. And what should we do with all this old furniture?
A: It ____________ (throw out)! I think the landlord should take care of that, though.

B Complete the blog with the correct form of *keep* and the verb in parentheses.

I ___keep having___ (have) technical problems. My computer ____________ (crash), and my printer ____________ (jam). I have to ____________ (put) a new battery into my mouse because it ____________ (die). The letters on my keyboard ____________ (stick), too. I ____________ (think) things will get better, but they just ____________ (get) worse. Time for some new electronics!

UNIT 7

1 Passive with prepositions page 45

- The prepositions *by, as a result of, because of, though,* and *due to* have similar meanings. They are used in sentences that describe cause and effect; they introduce the cause.

Match phrases from each column to make sentences. (More than one answer may be possible.)

Subject	Effect	Cause
1. The environment	is being contaminated due to	improper disposal of medical waste.
2. Our soil	is being harmed by	deforestation to make paper products.
3. Infectious diseases	are being endangered due to	hybrid cars.
4. Many different species	has been affected because of	the use of pesticides on fruits and vegetables.
5. Our air quality	has been reduced as a result of	the destruction of their habitats.
6. Smog pollution	have been spread through	climate changes like global warming.

2 Infinitive clauses and phrases page 47

- The form of *be* that follows the first infinitive must agree with the subject:
  The best way to reduce pollution **is** to improve public transportation.
  BUT The best ways to reduce homelessness **are** to build more public housing and provide free health care.

A Match the phrases.

1. What are the best ways to make _e_ **a.** people safer is to make the air healthier.
2. And the best way to do that is ___ **b.** to create a larger police force.
3. The best ways to reduce ___ **c.** people's quality of life is to help them feel safe.
4. One way to improve ___ **d.** air pollution are to ban cars and control industry.
5. Another way to make ___ **e.** this city a better place to live?

B Complete the conversation with the sentences above.

A: _What are the best ways to make this city a better place to live?_
B: Well, ___________________
A: That's right. ___________________
B: I agree. ___________________
A: Yes. Good air quality is key. ___________________
B: Maybe it's time to share our ideas with the mayor. Get out your phone.

UNIT 8

1 *Would rather* and *would prefer* page 51

- In negative statements with *would rather* and *would prefer*, the word *not* comes after the verbs: I'**d rather not**/I'**d prefer not** to take any courses this semester. (NOT: I ~~wouldn't rather~~/I ~~wouldn't prefer~~ to . . .)

Write questions and responses using the words in parentheses.

1. **A:** *Would you prefer to take classes during the day or at night?*
   (prefer / take classes / during the day / at night)
   B: ______
   (rather / take classes / at night)
2. **A:** ______
   (rather / study / business / education)
   B: ______
   (prefer / become / a teacher)
3. **A:** ______
   (prefer / sign up for / an art course / a computer course)
   B: ______
   (prefer / not / take / any classes this semester)
4. **A:** ______
   (rather / take up / an individual sport / a team sport)
   B: ______
   (rather / not / take up / either)

2 *By* + gerund to describe how to do things page 53

- In negative sentences that express comparison with *by* + gerund and *but*, *not* comes before *by*: A good way to improve your accent is **not by watching** TV **but by talking** to native speakers. In negative sentences with *by* that give advice without a comparison, *not* comes after *by*: A good way to improve your accent is **by not imitating** non-native speakers.

Combine the two ideas into one sentence using *by* + gerund.

1. You can build your vocabulary. Write down new words and expressions.
   One way to build your vocabulary is by writing down new words and expressions.
2. There is a good way to improve your accent. You can mimic native speakers.
   ______
3. Students can improve their listening skills. They can listen to English-language podcasts.
   ______
4. Hardworking students improve their grammar. They don't repeat common mistakes.
   ______
5. You can become fluent. Don't translate everything. Try to think in English.
   ______
6. You can become a good conversationalist. Don't just talk with others.
   Talk to yourself when you're alone, too.
   ______

UNIT 9

1 Get or have something done page 59

■ Sentences with *get/have* + object + past participle are passive. BUT Don't use any form of *be* before the past participle: Where can I **have** my watch **fixed**? (NOT: Where can I have my watch ~~be~~ fixed?)

Rewrite the statements as questions with *Where can I get/have . . . ?* Then complete B's answers with the information in parentheses.

1. I want to have someone shorten these pants.
   A: Where can I have these pants shortened?
   B: You can have them shortened at Tim's Tailoring. (at Tim's Tailoring)
2. I need to get someone to repair my computer.
   A: ______
   B: ______ (at Hackers Inc.)
3. I need to have someone prepare my taxes.
   A: ______
   B: ______ (by my accountant)
4. I'd like to get someone to cut my hair.
   A: ______
   B: ______ (at Beauty Barn)
5. I need to have someone paint my apartment.
   A: ______
   B: ______ (by Peter the Painter)

2 Making suggestions page 61

■ Use the base form of a verb – without *to* – after *Maybe you could . . .* and *Why don't you . . . ?*: Maybe you could **join** a book club. (NOT: Maybe you could ~~to~~ join a book club.) Why don't you **join** a book club? (NOT: Why don't you ~~to~~ join a book club?)

Complete the conversations with the correct form of the verbs in parentheses.

A: I'm having trouble meeting people here in the city. Any ideas?
B: I know it's hard. Why don't you ______ (join) a gym? That's usually a good place to meet people. Or maybe you could ______ (take) a class at the community college.
A: What about ______ (check out) the personal ads? Do you think that's a good way to meet people?
B: I wouldn't recommend doing that. People never tell the truth in those ads. But it might be a good idea ______ (find) a sports team. Have you thought about ______ (play) a team sport – maybe baseball or volleyball?
A: I'm not very good at most sports, but I used to play tennis.
B: There you go! One option is ______ (look up) tennis clubs in the city and see which clubs have teams people can join.
A: Now, that's a great idea. And I could always use the exercise!

UNIT 10

1 Referring to time in the past page 65

- Use *since* with a particular time: The UN has been in existence **since** 1945. Use *for* with a duration of time: The UN has been in existence **for** about the last 70 years.
- Use *in* and *during* with a specific period of time: Rock 'n' roll became popular **in/during** the 1950s.
- Use *from* and *to* to describe when something began and ended: World War II lasted **from** 1939 **to** 1945.

Complete the conversation with the words in the box. (Use some of the words more than once.)

ago	during	for	from	in	since	to

A: Hey, Dad. Did you use to listen to the Beatles?

B: Of course. In fact, I just listened to one of their records a few days *ago*. Do you realize that the Beatles's music has influenced other musicians ________ over 50 years? They were the greatest!

A: Well, I just found some interesting information about them. I'll read it to you: "The Beatles were a well-known British band ________ the 1960s. They performed together ________ 10 years – ________ 1960 ________ 1970. ________ 2003, the Beatles released *Let it Be*, even though one of the original members had been dead ________ 1980 and another had died ________ 2001. The original album had been recorded ________ 1969 and was in the studio safe ________ 34 years before the new, remixed album was released."

B: That *is* interesting. It's pretty amazing that people have listened to the Beatles ________ both the twentieth and the twenty-first centuries, isn't it?

2 Predicting the future with *will* page 67

- In sentences referring to time, the preposition *by* means "not later than." Don't confuse *by* with *within*, which means "some time during." Use *by* with points in time; use *within* with periods of time: **By** 2050, we will have eliminated starvation around the world. (NOT: ~~Within~~ 2050, . . .) **Within** the next five years, people will have invented mobile phone apps for nearly everything! (NOT: ~~By~~ the next five years, . . .)

Circle the correct verb forms to complete the conversation.

A: What do you think you **will do** / **will be doing** five years from now?

B: I'm not sure. Maybe I **will get** / **will have gotten** married by then. How about you?

A: I **will be finishing** / **will have finished** medical school, so I **will be doing** / **will have done** my internship five years from now.

B: So you **won't be living** / **won't have lived** around here in five years, I guess. Where do you think you **will live** / **will have lived**?

A: Wherever I get my internship.

UNIT 11

1 Time clauses page 73

- Use the past perfect in the main clause with *until* and *by the time*. This shows that one of the past events happened before the other: Until I got my driver's license, I **had** always **taken** public transportation. By the time I got my driver's license, all of my friends **had** already **gotten** theirs.

Circle the correct time expression to complete each sentence.

1. **After** / **(Until)** I traveled overseas, I hadn't known much about different cultures.
2. **After** / **Before** I got a full-time job, I had to live on a very limited budget.
3. **By the time** / **Once** I finished high school, I had already taken three college courses.
4. **As soon as** / **Before** I left for college, my mother turned my room into her office.
5. **Once** / **Until** I left home, I realized how much my family meant to me.
6. **By the time** / **The moment** you have a child, you feel totally responsible for him or her.

2 Expressing regret and describing hypothetical situations page 75

- Conditional sentences describing hypothetical situations often refer to both the present and the past:
  If **I'd finished** college, **I'd have** a better job now.
  past — present
  (NOT: If I'd finished college, I'd ~~have had~~ a better job now.)

A Write sentences with *should (not) have* to express regret about each person's situation.

1. Sarah was very argumentative with her teacher, so she had to stay after school.
   Sarah shouldn't have been argumentative with her teacher.
2. Ivan didn't save up for a car, so he still has to take public transportation.
   ______
3. Jon was very inactive when he was in college, so he gained a lot of weight.
   ______
4. Lisa didn't stay in touch with her high school classmates, so now she has very few friends.
   ______
5. Tony didn't study Spanish in school, so he's not bilingual now.
   ______

B Rewrite your sentences in part A, changing them to hypothetical situations.

1. If Sarah hadn't been argumentative with her teacher, she wouldn't have had to stay after school.
2. ______
3. ______
4. ______
5. ______

UNIT 12

1 Describing purpose page 79

- Don't use *for* immediately before an infinitive: **To have** a successful business, you need a lot of luck. (NOT: ~~For~~ to have a successful business, you need a lot of luck.)

A Complete the sentences with *in order to* or *in order for*.

1. ___In order for___ a supermarket to succeed, it has to be clean and well organized.
2. ________________ stay popular, a website needs to be accurate and visually attractive.
3. ________________ run a profitable furniture store, it's important to advertise on TV.
4. ________________ a restaurant to stay in business, it needs to have "regulars" – customers that come often.
5. ________________ establish a successful nail salon, it has to have a convenient location.
6. ________________ an online business to survive, it needs to have excellent pictures of the merchandise it's selling.

B Rewrite the sentences in part A without *In order*.

1. _For a supermarket to succeed, it has to be clean and well organized._
2. ____
3. ____
4. ____
5. ____
6. ____

2 Giving reasons page 81

- *Because* and *since* have the same meaning, and they can begin or end a sentence: **Because/Since** the food is always fantastic, Giorgio's is my favorite restaurant. = Giorgio's is my favorite restaurant **because/since** the food is always fantastic.
- Don't confuse *because* and *because of*. *Because* introduces an adverb clause and is followed by a subject and verb, while *because of* is a preposition and is followed by a noun object: **Because** Giorgio's is so popular, we should get there early. Giorgio's is popular **because of** its food and service.

Circle the correct words to complete the conversation.

A: I had to go downtown today **because** / **because of** / **due to** I needed to mail a package at the post office. **Due to** / **For** / **Since** I was only a few blocks from Main Street, I went over to Martin's. Did you know that Martin's has gone out of business? I'm so upset!

B: That's too bad, but I'm not surprised. A lot of family-owned shops are closing **because** / **because of** / **since** the construction of shopping malls.

A: Yeah, and don't forget about all the megastores that are popping up everywhere. **Because** / **For** / **The reason why** people prefer to shop there is to save money. Everyone loves a megastore **because** / **due to** / **since** the low prices and the huge selection.

B: Not me! I loved Martin's **for** / **since** / **the reason that** their beautiful clothes and friendly salespeople. When you were there, you almost felt like family. You'll never get that at a megastore!

UNIT 13

1 Past modals for degrees of certainty page 87

- Use the past modal *could have* to express possibility. BUT Use *couldn't have* when you are almost 100% sure something is impossible: I suppose he **could have gotten** stuck in traffic, but he **couldn't have forgotten** his own birthday party.

Complete the conversations with past modals *must (not) have, could (not) have,* or *may/might (not) have.* Use the degrees of certainty and the verbs in parentheses. (More than one answer may be possible.)

1. **A:** Yoko still hasn't called me back.
   B: She <u>might not have gotten</u> your message. (it's possible – not get)
2. **A:** What's wrong with Steven?
   B: Oh, you ______________________ the news. His dog ran away. (it's almost certain – not hear)
3. **A:** I went to see the Larsens today, but they didn't answer the door.
   B: Was their car there? If so, they ______________________ in the backyard. (it's possible – be)
4. **A:** Fabio said he was going to the party last night, but I didn't see him.
   B: Neither did I. He ______________________ there then. (it's not possible – not be)
5. **A:** I can't find my glasses, but I know I had them at work today.
   B: You ______________________ them at the office. (it's possible – leave)
6. **A:** Marc's new car looks really expensive.
   B: Yes, it does. It ______________________ a fortune! (it's almost certain – cost)

2 Past modals for judgments and suggestions page 89

- In advice with *would have*, the speaker means, "If I were you, . . ."

Read each situation and choose the corresponding judgment or suggestion for an alternative past action.

Situation

1. Sue forgot her boyfriend's birthday. <u>b</u>
2. Tim got a speeding ticket. ______
3. Ruth still hasn't paid me back. ______
4. Bill lied to us. ______
5. I spent an hour making Joe dinner, and he didn't even thank me. ______
6. Carol came over for dinner empty-handed. ______

Judgment/Suggestion

a. I wouldn't have lent her money.
b. She should have put it on her calendar.
c. He should have told the truth.
d. He shouldn't have gone over the limit.
e. She should have brought something.
f. I wouldn't have cooked for him.

UNIT 14

1 The passive to describe process page 93

- The modals *have to* and *need to* must agree with the subject; other modals, like *may be*, have only one form: Each character **has to/needs to** be drawn by the animators.

Put the words in the correct order to make sentences.

1. overnight / business / A / started / small / isn't / .
   A small business isn't started overnight.
2. to / plan / business / a / written / First, / be / has / .
3. research / Next, / done / be / market / should / .
4. needs / competition / to / the / Then / identified / be / .
5. online / ads / posted / be / Classified / may / .
6. work / are / employees / hired / can / start / the / so / Finally, / .

2 Defining and non-defining relative clauses page 96

- Use either *who* or *that* in defining relative clauses about people: A set designer is an artist **who/that** makes important contributions to a theater production. BUT Use only *who* in non-defining relative clauses about people: A set designer, **who** makes important contributions to a theater production, has to be very creative. (NOT: A set designer, ~~that~~ makes . . .)
- Use commas before and after a non-defining clause: A gossip columnist**,** who writes about celebrities and scandals**,** often gets to go to fabulous parties.

Combine these sentences with *who* or *that*. Add a comma wherever one is necessary.

1. A cartoon animator creates animated scenes for movies and games. He or she needs to have a high level of technical know-how.
   A cartoon animator, who needs to have a high level of technical know-how, creates animated scenes for movies and games.
2. A screenwriter is a talented person. He or she develops a story idea into a movie script.
   A screenwriter is a talented person that develops a story idea into a movie script.
3. Voice-over actors are usually freelancers. They give voice to characters in animated movies and video games.
4. Casting directors choose an actor for each part in a movie. They have usually been in the movie business for a long time.
5. High-budget movies always use big stars. The stars are known around the world.
6. Movie directors are greatly respected. They "make or break" a film.

UNIT 15

1 Giving recommendations and opinions page 101

■ *Ought to* has the same meaning as *should*, but it's more formal:
Traffic signs **ought to** be obeyed. = Traffic signs **should** be obeyed.

A student committee is discussing rules for their school. Complete speaker B's sentences with appropriate passive modals. (More than one answer is possible.)

1. **A:** Students must be required to clean off the cafeteria tables after lunch.
   B: I disagree. Students shouldn't be required to do that. That's what the cafeteria workers are paid to do.
2. **A:** Teachers shouldn't be allowed to park in the student parking lot.
   B: Why not? Teachers ________________ to park wherever a space is available. After all, they're here for us.
3. **A:** A rule has to be made to ban the use of cell phones in school.
   B: I don't think a rule ________________. Students may need their phones for emergency purposes.
4. **A:** Students mustn't be permitted to use calculators during math exams.
   B: Sometimes we ________________ to use them, especially when we're being tested on more complicated concepts than simple arithmetic.
5. **A:** Something has got to be done to control the noise in the hallways.
   B: Students ________________ to talk to each other between classes, though. They aren't disturbing anyone when classes aren't in session.
6. **A:** Teachers must be required to remind students about important exams.
   B: That's unnecessary. On the contrary, students ________________ to follow the syllabus and check important dates on the course websites.

2 Tag questions for opinions page 103

■ Tag questions added to statements in the simple present and simple past use the corresponding auxiliary verb in the tag: You **agree** with me, **don't** you? You **don't agree** with me, **do** you? You **paid** the rent, **didn't** you? You **didn't pay** the electric bill, **did** you?

Check (✓) the sentences if the tag questions are correct. If they're incorrect, write the correct tag questions.

1. Food is getting more and more expensive, ~~is it~~? isn't it
2. Supermarkets should try to keep their prices down, shouldn't they? ✓
3. People don't buy as many fresh fruits and vegetables as they used to, don't they? ________________
4. We have to buy healthy food for our children, don't we? ________________
5. Many children go to school hungry, won't they? ________________
6. Some people can't afford to eat meat every day, don't they? ________________
7. We can easily live without eating meat every day, can we? ________________
8. A lot of people are having a hard time making ends meet these days, haven't they? ________________

UNIT 16

1 Talking about past accomplishments page 107

■ When talking about past accomplishments and including a specific time, use the simple past – not the present perfect: I **was** able to complete my degree last year. (NOT: I~~'ve been~~ able to complete my degree last year.)

Complete the sentences about people's accomplishments. Use the verbs in parentheses. (More than one answer is possible.)

In the last 5 years, Ana . . .

1. managed to finish (finish) college.
2. ______________________ (pay) all her college loans.
3. ______________________ (start) her own company.
4. ______________________ (move) to the city.
5. ______________________ (make) some new friends.

In the past year, Bill . . .

6. ______________________ (buy) a new car.
7. ______________________ (take) a vacation.
8. ______________________ (get) a promotion at work.
9. ______________________ (learn) to cook.
10. ______________________ (visit) his grandparents in the south.

2 Describing goals and possible future accomplishments page 109

■ When talking about future accomplishments and goals, use *in* to refer to a period of time: I hope I'll find a new job **in** the next two months. Use *by* to talk about a time limit in the future: I hope I'll find a new job **by** the end of September. = I hope I'll find a new job not later than the end of September.

Complete the conversation. Use the verbs in parentheses. (Sometimes more than one answer is possible.)

Louise: So, Mike, what do you hope you will have accomplished (accomplish) five years from now?
Mike: I hope I ______________________ (complete) medical school, and I ______________________ (start) my residence in a good hospital.
Louise: What about your personal goals? What ______________________ (achieve) by then?
Mike: Well, I ______________________ (meet) that special someone, and, maybe, I ______________________ (get) married by then. What about you? What are your goals?
Louise: Well, I hope I ______________________ (finish) culinary school in the next five years, and I ______________________ (manage) to work with some famous chef.
Mike: Good plan! What about opening your own restaurant?
Louise: That will take some more time, but by the time I'm 35, I hope I ______________________ (open) my own bistro – Chez Louise.
Mike: I can hardly wait. I just love your food.

Grammar plus answer key

Unit 1

1 Relative pronouns

A: Ana, have you met Clint – the guy **X** Laurie is going to marry?
B: Oh, Clint and I have been friends for years. In fact, I'm the one **who/that** introduced Laurie and Clint.
A: Do you think they're right for each other?
B: Definitely. They're two people **who/that** have a lot in common – but not *too* much.
A: What does that mean?
B: Well, you don't want a partner **who/that** doesn't have his or her own interests. Couples **who/that** do everything together usually don't last very long.
A: I guess you're right, but the opposite isn't good, either. My last girlfriend was someone **X** I had nothing in common with. She wasn't the kind of girl **X** I could talk to easily.
B: Well, you can talk to *me* easily. . . .

2 *It* clauses + adverbial clauses with *when*

2. I hate it when I don't have enough time to study for an exam.
3. It doesn't bother me when friends talk to me about their problems.
4. It embarrasses me when I forget a co-worker's name.
5. I love it when my friends send me videos.
6. It upsets me when I have to wait for someone.

Unit 2

1 Gerund phrases

1. My brother's very interested in **becoming** a flight attendant. He dreams about **traveling** to new places.
2. I'm excited about **taking** a Japanese class next semester. I enjoy **learning** languages.
3. You wouldn't like **working** in a restaurant. You'd get tired of **standing** on your feet throughout the long shifts!
4. Our teacher is very good at **solving** problems. Maybe she should think about **changing** careers to become a guidance counselor.
5. **Making** a living as a photographer could be challenging. **Having** an impressive portfolio is really important to attract new clients and employers.

2 Comparisons

Answers may vary. Some possible answers:

2. A college professor earns more than an elementary school teacher.
3. Nurses have worse hours than psychiatrists.
4. Working as a police officer is as dangerous as being a firefighter.
5. A taxi driver isn't as well paid as an electrician.
6. Being a tour guide is less interesting than being an actor.

Unit 3

1 Requests with modals, *if* clauses, and gerunds

Answers may vary. Some possible answers:

2. A: Is it OK **if I use your computer?**
   B: You can use it, but please don't drink near it.
3. A: Would you mind **giving me a ride to class?**
   B: I'd be glad to. What time should I pick you up?
4. A: Can you **help me move on Saturday?**
   B: I'm sorry. I'm busy all weekend.
5. A: Would it be all right **if I had another piece of pie?**
   B: Yes, of course! Just pass me your plate.
6. A: Could you **lend me your red sweater?**
   B: Sorry. I don't like it when other people wear my clothes.

2 Indirect requests

2. Can you ask Susie if she wants to hang out with me?
3. Can you ask/tell Susie to text me?
4. Can you ask Susie if she knows my address?
5. Could you tell Susie not to forget to write?
6. Can you ask Susie what she's doing on Saturday?
7. Could you ask Susie if she has plans on Sunday?

Unit 4

1 Past continuous vs. simple past

1. A: How **did you break** your arm?
   B: It's a crazy story! Ramon and I **were riding** our bikes in the park when a cat **ran** out in front of me. I **was going** pretty fast, so when I **tried** to stop, I **went** off the road and **fell**.
   A: That's terrible! **Did you go** to the hospital after it **happened**?
   B: Yes. Luckily, we **weren't** too far from City Hospital, so we **went** there.
2. A: You'll never guess what **happened** to me this morning!
   B: What?
   A: Well, I **was brushing** my teeth when suddenly the water **went** off. I **had** toothpaste all over my mouth, and I couldn't wash it off.
   B: So what **did you do**?
   A: Fortunately, I **had** a big bottle of water in the refrigerator, so I **used** that water to rinse my mouth.

2 Past perfect

2. We had finished cleaning the house when our guests arrived.
3. Someone robbed my house yesterday because I had left the window open.
4. There was no food in the house because we had forgotten to stop at the supermarket.
5. I had called her three times when she finally answered.
6. I knew about the problem because your brother had told me about it.

Unit 5

1 Noun phrases containing relative clauses

2. a. Two things (that) I'd be very interested in are the food and the music.
   b. The food and the music are two things (that) I'd be very interested in.
3. a Something (that) I'd be worried about is not understanding the customs.
   b. Not understanding the customs is something (that) I'd be worried about.
4. a. Two people (who/that) I'd stay in touch with are my brother and sister.
   b. My brother and sister are two people (who/that) I'd stay in touch with.
5. a. One thing (that) I'd feel insecure about is speaking a new language.
   b. Speaking a new language is one thing (that) I'd feel insecure about.

2 Expectations

2. When a friend sends you an email, **you're expected to reply within a few days.**
3. If you want to visit someone, **it's not acceptable to show up without calling first.**
4. If you invite a married couple to dinner, **it's the custom for them to sit across from each other.**
5. When you go to a birthday party, **you're supposed to bring a gift.**

Unit 6

1 Describing problems 1

1. A: Oh, no! These jeans **have a tear** in them.
   B: And they **are stained**, too.
2. A: This table has **some damage** on top.
   B: I know. The wood **is scratched** because my son drags his toy cars on it.
3. A: Why are you drinking out of that glass? It **has a chip** in it.
   B: Oh, I didn't see it. That's why it **is leaking**.
4. A: Someone hit my car today. Look! The door **has a dent** in it.
   B: I see that. Your back light **is broken**, too.

5. A: I bought this blouse yesterday, but I have to take it back. There **is a hole** in it.
   B: It's really cute, but that's not the only problem. It **has a stain** on it, too.

2 Describing problems 2

A

A: Look at this place! A lot of work **needs to be done** before we move in.
B: You're not kidding. Let's make a list. First, the walls **need painting**.
A: Right. And the windows **need to be washed**. Add the rug to your list: It really **needs to be cleaned**. Do you think it **needs to be dry-cleaned**?
B: No, I think we can do it ourselves. It **needs shampooing**. We can rent a machine for that.
A: And what about the ceiling fan? I think it **needs to be replaced**. Fans aren't too expensive.
B: OK. I've added it to the list. And what should we do with all this old furniture?
A: It **needs to be thrown out**! I think the landlord should take care of that, though.

B

I **keep having** technical problems. My computer **keeps crashing**, and my printer **keeps jamming**. I have to **keep putting** a new battery into my mouse because it **keeps dying**. The letters on my keyboard **keep sticking**, too. I **keep thinking** things will get better, but they just **keep getting** worse. Time for some new electronics!

Unit 7

1 Passive with prepositions

Answers may vary. Some possible answers:

2. Our soil is being contaminated due to the use of pesticides on fruits and vegetables.
3. Infectious diseases have been spread through improper disposal of medical waste.
4. Many different species are being endangered due to the destruction of their habitats.
5. Our air quality has been affected because of deforestation to make paper products.
6. Smog pollution has been reduced as a result of hybrid cars.

2 Infinitive clauses and phrases

A

2. b 3. d 4. c 5. a

B

B: Well, **one way to improve people's quality of life is to help them feel safe.**
A: That's right. **And the best way to do that is to create a larger police force.**
B: I agree. **Another way to make people safer is to make the air healthier.**
A: Yes. Good air quality is key. **The best ways to reduce air pollution are to ban cars and control industry.**
B: Maybe it's time to share our ideas with the mayor. Get out your phone.

Unit 8

1 *Would rather* and *would prefer*

1. A: Would you prefer to take classes during the day or at night?
   B: I'd rather take classes at night.
2. A: Would you rather study business or education?
   B: I'd prefer to become a teacher.
3. A: Would you prefer to sign up for an art course or a computer course?
   B: I'd prefer not take any classes this semester.
4. A: Would you rather take up an individual sport or a team sport?
   B: I'd rather not take up either.

2 *By* + gerund to describe how to do things

2. A good way to improve your accent is by mimicking native speakers.
3. Students can improve their listening skills by listening to English-language podcasts.
4. Hardworking students improve their grammar by not repeating common mistakes.
5. You can become fluent not by translating everything but by trying to think in English.
6. You can become a good conversationalist not just by talking with others but by talking to yourself when you're alone, too.

Unit 9

1 Get or have something done

2. A: Where can I get/have my computer repaired?
   B: You can get/have it repaired at Hackers Inc.
3. A: Where can I get/have my taxes prepared?
   B: You can get/have them prepared by my accountant.
4. A: Where can I get/have my hair cut?
   B: You can get/have it cut at Beauty Barn.
5. A: Where can I get/have my apartment painted?
   B: You can get/have it painted by Peter the Painter.

2 Making suggestions

A: I'm having trouble meeting people here in the city. Any ideas?
B: I know it's hard. Why don't you **join** a gym? That's usually a good place to meet people. Or maybe you could **take** a class at the community college.
A: What about **checking out** the personal ads? Do you think that's a good way to meet people?
B: I wouldn't recommend doing that. People never tell the truth in those ads. But it might be a good idea **to find** a sports team. Have you thought about **playing** a team sport – maybe baseball or volleyball?
A: I'm not very good at most sports, but I used to play tennis.
B: There you go! One option is **to look up** tennis clubs in the city and see which clubs have teams people can join.
A: Now, that's a great idea. And I could always use the exercise!

Unit 10

1 Referring to time in the past

A: Hey, Dad. Did you use to listen to the Beatles?
B: Of course. In fact, I just listened to one of their records a few days **ago**. Do you realize that the Beatles's music has influenced other musicians **for** over 50 years? They were the greatest!
A: Well, I just found some interesting information about them. I'll read it to you: "The Beatles were a well-known British band **during/in** the 1960s. They performed together **for** 10 years – **from** 1960 **to** 1970. **In** 2003, the Beatles released a new version of their classic album *Let it Be*, even though one of the original members had been dead **since** 1980 and another had died **in** 2001. The original album had been recorded **in** 1969 and was in the studio safe **for** 34 years before the new, remixed album was released."
B: That *is* interesting. It's pretty amazing that people have listened to the Beatles **in** both the twentieth and the twenty-first centuries, isn't it?

2 Predicting the future with *will*

A: What do you think you **will be doing** five years from now?
B: I'm not sure. Maybe I **will have gotten** married by then. How about you?
A: I **will have finished** medical school, so I **will be doing** my internship five years from now.
B: So you **won't be living** around here in five years, I guess. Where do you think you **will live**?
A: Wherever I get my internship.

Unit 11

1 Time clauses

2. **Before** I got a full-time job, I had to live on a very limited budget.
3. **By the time** I finished high school, I had already taken three college courses.
4. **As soon as** I left for college, my mother turned my room into her office.
5. **Once** I left home, I realized how much my family meant to me.
6. **The moment** you have a child, you feel totally responsible for him or her.

2 Expressing regret and describing hypothetical situations

A

2. Ivan should have saved up for a car.
3. Jon shouldn't have been inactive when he was in college.
4. Lisa should have stayed in touch with her high school classmates.
5. Tony should have studied Spanish in school.

B

Answers may vary. Some possible answers:

2. If Ivan had saved up for a car, he wouldn't have to take public transportation.
3. If Jon hadn't been inactive when he was in college, he wouldn't have gained a lot of weight.
4. If Lisa had stayed in touch with her high school classmates, she wouldn't have very few friends.
5. If Tony had studied Spanish in school, he would be bilingual now.

Unit 12

1 Describing purpose

A

2. **In order to** stay popular, a website needs to be accurate and visually attractive.
3. **In order to** run a profitable furniture store, it's important to advertise on TV.
4. **In order for** a restaurant to stay in business, it needs to have "regulars" – customers that come often.
5. **In order to** establish a successful nail salon, it has to have a convenient location.
6. **In order for** an online business to survive, it needs to have excellent pictures of the merchandise it's selling.

B

2. To stay popular, a website needs to be accurate and visually attractive.
3. To run a profitable furniture store, it's important to advertise on TV.
4. For a restaurant to stay in business, it needs to have "regulars" – customers that come often.
5. To establish a successful nail salon, it has to have a convenient location.
6. For an online business to survive, it needs to have excellent pictures of the merchandise it's selling.

2 Giving reasons

A: I had to go downtown today **because** I needed to mail a package at the post office. **Since** I was only a few blocks from Main Street, I went over to Martin's. Did you know that Martin's has gone out of business? I'm so upset!
B: That's too bad, but I'm not surprised. A lot of family-owned shops are closing **because of** the construction of shopping malls.
A: Yeah, and don't forget about all the megastores that are popping up everywhere. **The reason why** people prefer to shop there is to save money. Everyone loves a megastore **due to** the low prices and the huge selection.
B: Not me! I loved Martin's **for** their beautiful clothes and friendly salespeople. When you were there, you almost felt like family. You'll never get that at a megastore!

Unit 13

1 Past modals for degrees of certainty

Answers may vary. Some possible answers:

2. A: What's wrong with Steven?
   B: Oh, you **must not have heard** the news. His dog ran away.
3. A: I went to see the Larsens today, but they didn't answer the door.
   B: Was their car there? If so, they **could have been** in the backyard.
4. A: Fabio said he was going to the party last night, but I didn't see him.
   B: Neither did I. He **couldn't have been** there then.
5. A: I can't find my glasses, but I know I had them at work today.
   B: You **might have left** them at the office.
6. A: Marc's new car looks really expensive.
   B: Yes, it does. It **must have cost** a fortune!

2 Past modals for judgments and suggestions

2. d 3. a 4. c 5. f 6. e

Unit 14

1 The passive to describe process

2. First, a business plan has to be written.
3. Next, market research should be done.
4. Then the competition needs to be identified.
5. Classified ads may be posted online.
6. Finally, employees are hired so the work can start.

2 Defining and non-defining relative clauses

3. Voice-over actors, who give voice to characters in animated movies and video games, are usually freelancers.
4. Casting directors, who have usually been in the movie business for a long time, choose an actor for each part in a movie.
5. High-budget movies always use big stars that are known around the world.
6. Movie directors, who "make or break" a film, are greatly respected.

Unit 15

1 Giving recommendations and opinions

Answers may vary. Some possible answers:

2. A: Teachers shouldn't be allowed to park in the student parking lot.
   B: Why not? Teachers **should be allowed** to park wherever a space is available. After all, they're here for us.
3. A: A rule has to be made to ban the use of cell phones in school.
   B: I don't think a rule **has to be made**. Students may need their phones for emergency purposes.
4. A: Students mustn't be permitted to use calculators during math exams.
   B: Sometimes we **should be permitted** to use them, especially when we're being tested on more complicated concepts than simple arithmetic.
5. A: Something has got to be done to control the noise in the hallways.
   B: Students **should be allowed** to talk to each other between classes, though. They aren't disturbing anyone when classes aren't in session.
6. A: Teachers must be required to remind students about important exams.
   B: That's unnecessary. On the contrary, students **should be required** to follow the syllabus and check important dates on the course websites.

2 Tag questions for opinions

3. do they
4. ✓
5. don't they
6. can they
7. can't we
8. aren't they

Unit 16

1 Talking about past accomplishments

Answers may vary. Some possible answers:

2. has managed to pay
3. has been able to start
4. was able to move
5. managed to make
6. was able to buy
7. has managed to take
8. has managed to get
9. has been able to learn
10. has managed to visit

2 Describing goals and possible future accomplishments

Louise: So, Mike, what do you hope you will have accomplished five years from now?
Mike: I hope I**'ll have completed** medical school and I**'ll have started / 'd like to have started** my residence in a good hospital.
Louise: What about your personal goals? What **would you like to have achieved** by then?
Mike: Well, I**'d like to have met** that special someone, and, maybe I**'ll have gotten** married by then. What about you? What are your goals?
Louise: Well, I hope I**'ll have finished** culinary school in five years, and I**'ll have managed / 'd like to have managed** to work with some famous chef.
Mike: Good plan! What about opening your own restaurant?
Louise: That will take some more time, but by the time I'm 35, I hope I**'ll have opened** my own bistro – Chez Louise.
Mike: I can hardly wait. I just love your food.

Credits

The authors and publishers acknowledge the following sources of copyright material and are grateful for the permissions granted. While every effort has been made, it has not always been possible to identify the sources of all the material used, or to trace all copyright holders. If any omissions are brought to our notice, we will be happy to include the appropriate acknowledgements on reprinting and in the next update to the digital edition, as applicable.

Key: Ex = Exercise, T = Top, B = Below, C = Centre, CR = Centre Right, TR = Top Right, BR = Below Right, TL = Top Left, TC = Top Centre, BL = Below Left, BC = Below Centre, L = Left, R = Right, CL = Centre Left, B/G = Background.

Illustrations

Mark Duffin: 39, 115, 119, 120; **Thomas Girard** (Good Illustration): 86; **Dusan Lakicevic** (Beehive Illustration): 18, 24; **Gavin Reece** (New Division): 43.

Photos

Back cover (woman with whiteboard): Jenny Acheson/Stockbyte/GettyImages; Back cover (whiteboard): Nemida/GettyImages; Back cover (man using phone): Betsie Van Der Meer/Taxi/GettyImages; Back cover (woman smiling): PeopleImages.com/DigitalVision/GettyImages; Back cover (name tag): Tetra Images/GettyImages; Back cover (handshake): David Lees/Taxi/GettyImages; p. v (TL): Hill Street Studios/Blend Images/GettyImages; p. v (BR): Hill Street Studios/Blend Images/GettyImages; p. v (BL): track5/E+/GettyImages; p. v (TR): fstop123/E+/GettyImages; p. 2 (header), p. vi (Unit 1): Tony Anderson/Taxi/GettyImages; p. 2 (T): Steve West/Taxi Japan/GettyImages; p. 2 (B): PhotoInc/E+/GettyImages; p. 4 (CR): Thomas Barwick/Iconica/GettyImages; p. 4 (BR): monkeybusinessimages/GettyImages; p. 5 (T): Shawna Hansen/Moment Open/GettyImages; p. 5 (B): Andersen Ross/Stockbyte/GettyImages; p. 6: Caiaimage/Tom Merton/OJO+/Cultura/GettyImages; p. 7: Heath Korvola/Stone/GettyImages; p. 8 (header), p. vi (Unit 2): Kelvin Murray/Taxi/GettyImages; p. 8 (TR): Paul Bradbury/Caiaimage/GettyImages; p. 8 (Lia): Tetra Images/Brand X Pictures/GettyImages; p. 8 (Josh): NicolasMcComber/E+/GettyImages; p. 8 (Ed): XiXinXing/GettyImages; p. 8 (Rose): Tim Robberts/The Image Bank/GettyImages; p. 8 (Jeff): T2 Images/Cultura/GettyImages; p. 8 (Mei): Yagi Studio/DigitalVision/GettyImages; p. 8 (Anna): Ron Levine/DigitalVision/GettyImages; p. 8 (Mike): Jon Feingersh/Blend Images/GettyImages; p. 9 (student): Nycretoucher/Stone/GettyImages; p. 9 (volunteer): asiseeit/E+/GettyImages; p. 9 (business): Thomas Barwick/Stone/GettyImages; p. 9 (movie set): bjones27/E+/GettyImages; p. 10: Sue Barr/Image Source/GettyImages; p. 11: JP Greenwood/The Image Bank/GettyImages; p. 12: Edge Magazine/Future/Future Publishing/GettyImages; p. 13 (T): Gary Burchell/Taxi/GettyImages; p. 13 (C): Hero Images/GettyImages; p. 13 (B): asiseeit/E+/GettyImages; p. 14: Juanmonino/E+/GettyImages; p. 15 (CR): Hero Images/GettyImages; p. 15 (BR): kali9/E+/GettyImages; p. 16 (header), p. iv (Unit 3): Ascent Xmedia/Stone/GettyImages; p. 16 (T): PeopleImages/DigitalVision/Getty Images Plus/GettyImages; p. 16 (B): Tetra Images/GettyImages; p. 17: Maskot/GettyImages; p. 18 (Sara): Tim Robberts/Taxi/GettyImages; p. 18 (Kim): monkeybusinessimages/iStock/Getty Images Plus/GettyImages; p. 19 (T): Maskot/Maskot/GettyImages; p. 19 (Ex 9): Tetra Images-Rob Lewine/Brand X Pictures/Getty Images; p. 20: Roy Mehta/Iconica/GettyImages; p. 21: Tetra Images/GettyImages; p. 22 (header), p. iv (Unit 4): Tom Merton/Caiaimage/GettyImages; p. 22 (news): Rune Johansen/Photolibrary/GettyImages; p. 22 (health): Peter Dazeley/Photographer's Choice/GettyImages; p. 22 (trending topics): Jess Nichols/EyeEm/GettyImages; p. 22 (arts): Daniel Allan/Cultura/GettyImages; p. 22 (science): Don Klumpp/The Image Bank/GettyImages; p. 22 (tech): Georgijevic/E+/GettyImages; p. 23: Tetra Images/Brand X Pictures/GettyImages; p. 25: Rachel Lewis/Lonely Planet Images/GettyImages; p. 25 (Carol): Jetta Productions/Blend Images/GettyImages; p. 25 (Milo): JohnnyGreig/E+/GettyImages; p. 26: elvira_gumirova/GettyImages; p. 26 (B/G): Anna Bryukhanova/GettyImages; p. 27: artpipi/E+/GettyImages; p. 28: JGI/Jamie Grill/Blend Images/GettyImages; p. 29: Matt Dutile/Image Source/GettyImages; p. 30 (header), p. iv (Unit 5): Image Source/DigitalVision/GettyImages; p. 30 (T): William King/Taxi/GettyImages; p. 30 (B): PBNJ Productions/Blend Images/GettyImages; p. 31: Buena Vista Images/DigitalVision/GettyImages; p. 32: Nachosuch/iStock/Getty Images Plus/GettyImages; p. 33: John Fedele/Blend Images/GettyImages; p. 34 (T): Dave & Les Jacobs/Blend Images/GettyImages; p. 34 (B): Kay Chernush/Stockbyte/GettyImages; p. 35 (B): Westend61/GettyImages; p. 35 (TR): Rafael Elias/Moment/GettyImages; p. 36 (header), p. vi (Unit 6): Caiaimage/Trevor Adeline/Caiaimage/GettyImages; p. 36 (CR): Peter Cade/The Image Bank/GettyImages; p. 37 (photo 1): p6opov/iStock/Getty Images Plus/GettyImages; p. 37 (photo 2): Michael Blann/DigitalVision/GettyImages; p. 37 (photo 3): Shannon Miller/Moment/GettyImages; p. 37 (photo 4): xril/iStock/Getty Images Plus/GettyImages; p. 38 (TR): Creatas/Creatas/Getty Images Plus/GettyImages; p. 38 (BR): Mel Yates/Photodisc/Getty Images Plus/GettyImages; p. 38 (Leory): Monty Rakusen/Cultura/GettyImages; p. 38 (Heather): Sam Edwards/Caiaimage/GettyImages; p. 40: Jupiterimages/PHOTOS.com/Getty Images Plus/GettyImages; p. 41: Image Source/GettyImages; p. 42: Jamie Grill/GettyImages; p. 43: Klaus Vedfelt/DigitalVision/GettyImages; p. 44 (header), p. vi (Unit 7): Hero Images/GettyImages; p. 44 (B): Todd Wright/Blend Images/GettyImages; p. 45 (TL): narvikk/E+/GettyImages; p. 45 (TC): TongRo Images Inc/TongRo Images/GettyImages; p. 45 (TR): Visuals Unlimited, Inc./Thomas Marent/Visuals Unlimited/GettyImages; p. 45 (BL): mshch/iStock/Getty Images Plus/GettyImages; p. 45 (BC): Marcos Alves/Moment/GettyImages; p. 45 (BR): Helmut Meyer zur Capellen/imageBROKER/Getty Images Plus/GettyImages; p. 46: Michael Krasowitz/Photographer's Choice/GettyImages; p. 47: Photofusion/Universal Images Group/GettyImages; p. 48 (TL): jinga80/iStock/Getty Images Plus/GettyImages; p. 48 (TR): sestovic/E+/GettyImages; p. 48 (BL): 101cats/iStock/Getty Images Plus/GettyImages; p. 48 (BR): inFocusDC/iStock/Getty Images Plus/GettyImages; p. 49 (TR): Cigdem Sean Cooper/Moment Open/GettyImages; p. 49 (BL): Antonio Busiello/robertharding/GettyImages; p. 50 (header), p. vi (Unit 8): akindo/DigitalVision Vectors/GettyImages; p. 51: Hill Street Studios/Blend Images/GettyImages; p. 52: Wavebreakmedia Ltd/Wavebreak Media/Getty Images Plus/GettyImages; p. 53: MarioGuti/iStock/Getty Images Plus/GettyImages; p. 54 (T): Dave & Les Jacobs/Blend Images/Getty Images Plus/GettyImages; p. 54 (B): JGI/Jamie Grill/Blend Images/GettyImages; p. 55: Apeloga AB/Cultura/GettyImages; p. 56: John Lund/DigitalVision/GettyImages; p. 57: mediaphotos/iStock/Getty Images Plus/GettyImages; p. 58 (header), p. viii (Unit 9): Dusty Pixel photography/Moment/GettyImages; p. 58 (automotive): Reza Estakhrian/Iconica/GettyImages; p. 58 (car wash): gilaxia/E+/iStock/Getty Images Plus/GettyImages; p. 58 (computer repair): Tetra Images/GettyImages; p. 58 (security repair): fatihhoca/iStock/Getty Images Plus/GettyImages; p. 58 (carpet cleaning): leezsnow/E+/GettyImages; p. 58 (home repair): sturti/E+/GettyImages; p. 58 (laundry cleaning): kali9/E+/GettyImages; p. 58 (tutoring): Hill Street Studios/Blend Images/GettyImages; p. 59 (Jessica): imagenavi/GettyImages; p. 59 (Peter): g-stockstudio/iStock/Getty Images Plus/GettyImages; p. 59 (Barry): Maskot/GettyImages; p. 59 (Tricia): Andersen Ross/GettyImages; p. 60: MachineHeadz/iStock/Getty Images Plus/GettyImages; p. 61: Morsa Images/DigitalVision/GettyImages; p. 62 (L): James And James/Photolibrary/GettyImages; p. 62 (C): Jose Luis Pelaez Inc/Blend Images/GettyImages; p. 62 (R): Dan Dalton/Caiaimage/GettyImages; p. 63: Paul Morigi/Getty Images Entertainment/Getty Images North America/GettyImages; p. 64 (header), p. viii (Unit 10): Kimberley Coole/Lonely Planet Images/GettyImages; p. 64 (1975): Jason Todd/DigitalVision/GettyImages; p. 64 (1982): Photofusion/Universal Images Group Editorial/GettyImages; p. 64 (1996): Kimberly Butler/The LIFE Images Collection/GettyImages; p. 64 (2004): Graffizone/E+/GettyImages; p. 64 (2006): Future Publishing/Future/GettyImages; p. 64 (2013): Jacob Ammentorp Lund/iStock/Getty Images Plus/GettyImages; p. 65 (T): Mark Dadswell/Getty Images Sport/Getty Images AsiaPac/GettyImages; p. 65 (B): andresr/E+/GettyImages; p. 66: Steve Sands/FilmMagic/GettyImages; p. 67 (T): Walter Bibikow/AWL Images/GettyImages; p. 67 (B): ferrantraite/Vetta/GettyImages; p. 68 (BR): JGI/Jamie Grill/Blend Images/GettyImages; p. 68 (crossing slackline): Ascent Xmedia/The Image Bank/GettyImages; p. 69 (B/G): vladimir zakharov/Moment/GettyImages; p. 69: PASIEKA/Science Photo Library/GettyImages; p. 70: Jonas Gratzer/LightRocket/GettyImages; p. 71 (T): NASA/The LIFE Picture Collection/GettyImages; p. 71 (B): Hero Images/GettyImages; p. 72 (header), p. viii (Unit 11): Hero Images/GettyImages; p. 72 (T): PeopleImages/DigitalVision/GettyImages; p. 72 (B): Hero Images/GettyImages; p. 73: martinedoucet/E+/GettyImages; p. 74: Jamie Kingham/Image Source/GettyImages; p. 75 (L): Rick Gomez/Blend Images/GettyImages; p. 75 (R): Simon Winnall/Taxi/GettyImages; p. 76: Elenathewise/iStock/Getty Images Plus/GettyImages; p. 77 (R): FilippoBacci/E+/GettyImages; p. 77 (L): Comstock Images/Stockbyte/GettyImages; p. 78 (header), p. viii (Unit 12): Jose Luis Pelaez Inc/Blend Images/GettyImages; p. 78: Martin Barraud/Caiaimage/GettyImages; p. 79: Martin Poole/The Image Bank/GettyImages; p. 80 (T): Tim Robberts/GettyImages; p. 80 (B): Chris Ryan/Caiaimage/GettyImages;

p. 81: Anadolu Agency/Anadolu/GettyImages; p. 82: Car Culture/Car Culture®Collection/GettyImages; p. 83 (T): UpperCut Images/GettyImages; p. 84: Tetra Images/GettyImages; p. 85: ullstein bild/GettyImages; p. 86 (header), p. viii (Unit 13): Manfred Gottschalk/Lonely Planet Images/GettyImages; p. 86: Image Source/GettyImages; p. 87 (L): James Lauritz/Photodisc/GettyImages; p. 87 (R): RichLegg/E+/GettyImages; p. 88 (T): Sweet Wedding/GettyImages; p. 88 (B): Gogosvm/iStock/Getty Images Plus/GettyImages; p. 89: LisaValder/E+/GettyImages; p. 91 (T): serdjophoto/iStock/Getty Images Plus/GettyImages; p. 91 (B): Ian Cuming/Ikon Images/GettyImages; p. 92 (header), p. viii (Unit 14): bjones27/E+/GettyImages; p. 92 (BR): GUILLAUME SOUVANT/AFP/GettyImages; p. 93 (T): GUILLAUME SOUVANT/AFP/GettyImages; p. 93 (B): Highwaystarz-Photography/iStock/Getty Images Plus/GettyImages; p. 94 (TL): B. O'Kane/Alamy; p. 94 (TC): Hill Street Studios/Blend Images/GettyImages; p. 94 (TR): Tom and Steve/Moment/GettyImages; p. 94 (CL): Daniela White Images/Moment/GettyImages; p. 94 (C): Lucia Lambriex/Taxi/GettyImages; p. 94 (CR): Caiaimage/Sam Edwards/OJO+/GettyImages; p. 94 (B): Hero Images/GettyImages; p. 95 (TL): Mads Perch/Iconica/GettyImages; p. 95 (TR): Plume Creative/DigitalVision/GettyImages; p. 95 (BL): Sam Edwards/Caiaimage/GettyImages; p. 95 (BR): asiseeit/E+/GettyImages; p. 96: Gary Houlder/Taxi/GettyImages; p. 97 (R): FREDERICK FLORIN/AFP/GettyImages; p. 97 (L): Tim Robberts/The Image Bank/GettyImages; p. 98: Image Source/GettyImages; p. 99 (TL): Vico Collective/Michael Shay/Blend Images/GettyImages; p. 99 (TR): Eric Audras/ONOKY/GettyImages; p. 99 (BR): Morsa Images/DigitalVision/GettyImages; p. 100 (header), p. viii (Unit 15): 04linz/iStock/GettyImages; p. 100: Joe McBride/Stone/GettyImages; p. 101: Boston Globe/GettyImages; p. 102 (T): Toby Burrows/DigitalVision/GettyImages; p. 102 (B): andipantz/iStock/GettyImages; p. 103: Maskot/GettyImages; p. 104: John Lund/Marc Romanelli/Blend Images/GettyImages; p. 105: Commercial Eye/The Image Bank/GettyImages; p. 106 (header), p. viii (Unit 16): David Trood/Stone/GettyImages; p. 106 (T): Hero Images/GettyImages; p. 106 (B/G): Klaus Vedfelt/DigitalVision/GettyImages; p. 106 (B): Tetra Images - Daniel Grill/Brand X Pictures/GettyImages; p. 107: Tara Moore/Taxi/GettyImages; p. 108: Ariel Skelley/Blend Images/GettyImages; p. 109 (T): Lumina Images/Blend Images/GettyImages; p. 109 (B): Nino H. Photography/Moment Open/GettyImages; p. 110 (TL): David Malan/Photographer's Choice/GettyImages; p. 110 (TC): Sam Edwards/OJO Images/GettyImages; p. 110 (TR): m-imagephotography/iStock/Getty Images Plus/GettyImages; p. 110 (BR): John S Lander/LightRocket/GettyImages; p. 111 (T): Samir Hussein/WireImage/GettyImages; p. 111 (B): AFP/GettyImages; p. 112: Zero Creatives/Image Source/GettyImages; p. 113: andresrimaging/iStock/Getty Images Plus/GettyImages; p. 115 (Gaston): Serge Krouglikoff/The Image Bank/GettyImages; p. 115 (Melissa): Sam Edwards/OJO Images/GettyImages; p. 115 (Don): Neustockimages/E+/GettyImages; p. 115 (Emma): Tom Werner/Taxi/GettyImages; p. 115 (Mike): Hero Images/GettyImages; p. 115 (Paola): filadendron/E+/GettyImages; p. 115 (Joanne): digitalskillet/iStock/Getty Images Plus/GettyImages; p. 115 (Ren): Stewart Cohen/Taxi/GettyImages; p. 116 (TL): Bluemoon Stock/Stockbyte/GettyImages; p. 116 (TC): scanrail/iStock/Getty Images Plus/GettyImages; p. 116 (TR): sihuo0860371/iStock/Getty Images Plus/GettyImages; p. 116 (CL): Comstock/Stockbyte/GettyImages; p. 116 (C): EasyBuy4u/E+/GettyImages; p. 116 (CR): Rebekah Logan/Moment Mobile/GettyImages; p. 116 (BL): JosT Elias/Hemera/Getty Images Plus/GettyImages; p. 116 (BC): Zoonar RF/Zoonar/Getty Images Plus/GettyImages; p. 116 (BR): tiler84/iStock/Getty Images Plus/GettyImages; p. 118 (TL): Yellow Dog Productions/The Image Bank/GettyImages; p. 118 (TR): Cultura Exclusive/MoofCultura Exclusive/GettyImages; p. 118 (BL): Alix Minde/PhotoAlto Agency RF Collections/GettyImages; p. 121: Pete Marovich/Getty Images News/Getty Images North America/GettyImages; p. 122: Michael Marquand/Lonely Planet Images/GettyImages; p. 123 (TL): Tetra Images/GettyImages; p. 123 (BR): doble-d/iStock/Getty Images Plus/GettyImages; p. 124 (Frida Kahlo): Michael Ochs Archives/GettyImages; p. 124 (Volkswagen): 8c061bbf_466/iStock Editorial/Getty Images Plus/GettyImages; p. 124 (Alexander): Bettmann/GettyImages; p. 125 (R): jmb_studio/iStock/Getty Images Plus/GettyImages; p. 125 (L): jmb_studio/iStock/Getty Images Plus/GettyImages; p. 125 (backpack): Songbird839/iStock/Getty Images Plus/GettyImages; p. 125 (dollar jar): IcemanJ/iStock/Getty Images Plus/GettyImages; p. 125 (balls): Ian McKinnell/Photographer's Choice/GettyImages; p. 125 (chips): MarkGillow/E+/GettyImages; p. 125 (video game): Angelo Angeles/Hemera/Getty Images Plus/GettyImages; p. 126 (L): Stuart Dee/Photographer's Choice/GettyImages; p. 126 (C): Riccardo Livorni/EyeEm/GettyImages; p. 126 (R): 3D_generator/iStock/Getty Images Plus/GettyImages; p. 127: Daviles/iStock/Getty Images Plus/GettyImages; p. 128 (photo 1a): Carl Court/Getty Images News/Getty Images Europe/GettyImages; p. 128 (photo 1b): Helen H. Richardson/Denver Post/GettyImages; p. 128 (photo 2a): GabryC/iStock/Getty Images Plus/GettyImages; p. 128 (photo 2b): Tom Merton/Hoxton/GettyImages; p. 128 (photo 3a): Multi-bits/The Image Bank/GettyImages; p. 128 (photo 3b): Stuart O'Sullivan/The Image Bank/GettyImages; p. 128 (photo 4a): scyther5/iStock/Getty Images Plus/GettyImages; p. 128 (photo 4b): Bread and Butter Productions/The Image Bank/GettyImages; p. 129 (TR): Dave J Hogan/Getty Images Entertainment/Getty Images Europe/GettyImages; p. 129 (CL): Dan Istitene/Getty Images Sport/Getty Images Europe/GettyImages; p. 129 (CR): Allen Berezovsky/WireImage/GettyImages; p. 129 (BL): Fred Stein Archive/Archive Photos/GettyImages; p. 129 (BR): Bettmann/GettyImages; p. 130 (L): Image Source/GettyImages; p. 130 (C): Jen Grantham/iStock Editorial/Getty Images Plus/GettyImages; p. 130 (R): Mauro Speziale/The Image Bank/GettyImages; p. 131: Jay Reilly/UpperCut Images/GettyImages.